Annabel Karmel's
QUICK CHILDREN'S MEALS

Over 170 healthy new recipe ideas
for the whole family to enjoy

Illustrated by Susan Hellard

EBURY PRESS
LONDON

3 5 7 9 10 8 6 4 2
Text copyright © Annabel Karmel 1997
Illustrations © Susan Hellard 1997
Back cover and inside photograph © Harry Ormisher 1997

First published in the United Kingdom in 1997 by
Ebury Press
Random House · 20 Vauxhall Bridge Road · London SW1V 2SA

Random House Australia (Pty) Limited
20 Alfred Street · Milsons Point · Sydney · New South Wales 2061 · Australia

Random House New Zealand Limited
18 Poland Road · Glenfield · Auckland 10 · New Zealand

Random House South Africa (Pty) Limited
Endulini, 5A Jubilee Road, Parktown 2193, South Africa

Random House Canada
1265 Aerowood Drive · Mississauga · Ontario L4W 1B9

Random House UK Limited Reg. No. 954009
A CIP catalogue record for this book is available from the British Library.

ISBN 0 09 185189 0

Designed by Martin Lovelock
Printed and bound in Portugal by Printer Portuguesa L.d.a.

Papers used by Ebury Press are natural recyclable products made from wood grown in sustainable forests.

CONTENTS

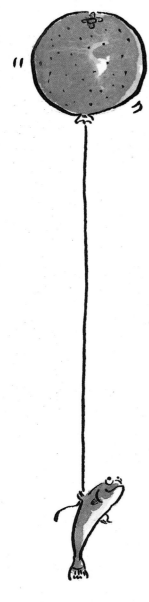

To Nicholas, Lara and Scarlett – the three most important reasons for my writing this book.

INTRODUCTION

This is a book for everyday family eating. The recipes are quick and easy to prepare and use fresh, healthy foods. The list of ingredients for each recipe is short and many of the ingredients are likely to be in your fridge or larder already.

One of the most important tasks in every mother's routine involves preparing food two and sometimes three times a day and as a working mother of three boisterous young children, Nicholas 8, Lara 7 and Scarlett 5, I know how difficult it can be to find the time to make a home-cooked meal.

The recipes in this book are designed to appeal to those parents who lack the time to cook but want the family to enjoy eating fresh, tasty and healthy meals without resorting to heavily-processed convenience foods.

Since children's health depends so much on their diet, it's not surprising that parents worry about what their child is eating. However, very often the problem is not so much getting your child to eat but how to resist the junk and convenience foods. Burgers, pizzas, crisps, sweets and fizzy drinks are so appealing to children but fill them up without providing them with the nutrients that they need. The diet of many children today is a recipe for a future disaster. Children who have got used to eating highly-processed foods with lots of saturated fat, added sugar and salt will crave these foods for the rest of their lives. They could be sowing the seeds for coronary heart disease later in life, particularly if there is a family history of heart disease or obesity. This book aims to steer the whole family in the right direction both food-wise and fun-wise. Establishing good eating habits in childhood will set your child up for a healthy life ahead.

Rejection of food that has been prepared with love and care is hurtful so I have tested each of the recipes in this book on a panel of discerning and fussy children (not only my own, since they might be accused of not being totally unbiased) to try to capture that balance between health and nutrition and taste and child appeal. There are lots of delicious and quick ideas to make your own healthy fast food – chicken sausages made with finely chopped onion and grated apple, a quick and easy pizza base topped with tasty vegetables and cheese, frozen yogurt ice cream and ice lollies made from fresh fruit. There are also many cunning ways to disguise ingredients that your child might normally refuse to eat.

Fast food however is not just about pizzas and hamburgers. It's fun for children to expand their repertoire and not be conditioned into only eating the same old foods whether it be school lunches, a trip to McDonalds or a take-away pizza. Introduce children to salmon teriyaki, grilled chicken on a skewer, spaghetti with vegetables or delicious homemade soups. Children always used to eat the same as their parents but now it seems real food is reserved for adults only. The label 'suitable for children' has, unbelievably, come to represent in many cases some of the worst quality, most unhealthy food on offer. The family recipes in my book range from 10-minute meals to 'Relax While It Cooks' meals that are easy to prepare and cook in the oven while you can get on with important matters like supervising homework!

Recently, supermarkets have begun stocking a much wider and more international range of foods. Many of these can be used to make wonderful recipes to stimulate the taste buds and widen the horizons of your child's diet. In this book, there is a collection of tempting oriental recipes; like 10-Minute Prawn Stir Fry, Yakitori Chicken and Chinese Noodles with Beansprouts which I have found to be particularly popular with children. There is a chapter on cooking an entire meal from scratch in a microwave, which is not only quick and easy but also surprisingly successful. If like me your use of the microwave is normally limited to reheating foods, give it a whirl. I have also included some slightly more grown-up recipes which are personal favourites and which would be ideal for special occasions and entertaining. The majority of the recipes are marked suitable for freezing so when you come home tired and hungry after a long day you can reach into your freezer for a delicious home-cooked meal.

Dessert for my family is nearly always a selection of fresh fruit, but there are times when you will want to bake a cake or treat your family to a delicious pudding and these can be a useful source of calories for a growing child. Hopefully you will be inspired by my collection of truly delicious *quick* and *easy* cakes and desserts.

Tasty, appealing and nutritious home-cooked food where you have selected all the ingredients is definitely a positive contribution to laying the foundations of a healthy lifestyle. Put your heart into this home-cooking business since there really is nothing more gratifying than seeing the whole family tucking in to your labour of love.

I'm really pleased to produce this fourth book – it's a little like having a new baby but without the nappy changing!

Go on, enjoy yourself and Bon Appétit!

RECOMMENDED GUIDELINES FOR FEEDING YOUR CHILD

Children need calories to grow as well as an adequate supply of protein, vitamins and minerals. This is best provided by offering children a good varied diet. Although a low fat, high fibre diet is fine for adults, it is not appropriate for young children. As children grow older, they can adopt a more adult type diet.

Starchy foods like bread, pasta, rice, potato and cereals should make up the major part of your child's diet, together with protein foods such as lean meat, chicken, fish, eggs or dairy products and plenty of fresh vegetables and fruit.

Milk is an important source of calories and calcium. Children under five should drink at least ⅔ of a pint a day of whole milk or eat the equivalent in dairy products like cheese or yogurt.

Eggs should be served to young children with the white and yolk cooked until solid.

Whole nuts should not be given to children under the age of five because of the risk of choking. Peanut butter and finely ground nuts are fine from 8 months, provided there is no family history of allergy. Obviously, children who react to nuts should avoid all sources of nuts including oils.

Always make sure there are no bones when serving fish to children.

Do not add salt or salty products like soy sauce or stock cubes for children under one year. After that time, you can add some salt to foods but do not use excessive amounts.

All servings are adult portions. You will know your own children's appetites best but allow approximately half an adult portion per child.

All recipes in this book are suitable for children from one year.

BRIGHT-EYED BREAKFASTS

The Best Breakfast Food

The first meal of the day is also the most important and when you give your child breakfast, you're setting him up for his day at school. Children have high energy and nutrient requirements so try to make sure that they have a good balanced breakfast every morning. Here's how to make sure your child gets that crucial breakfast boost.

1. Fruit and Fruit Juice
Experiment with a wide variety of seasonal fruits. Try two salads like mango, peach and strawberry. Berry and citrus fruits are particularly good in your child's diet. Vitamin C helps to boost immunity, so fresh fruit and juice are excellent.

2. Grains, Nuts, Seeds and Bread
If your child is hooked on sugar-coated cereals, then try mixing them with wholegrain low-sugar cereals like bran flakes, Shreddies, cornflakes or muesli. Nuts (for older children) and seeds also contain important nutrients and will help your child to absorb the calcium in his food, so adding foods like sunflower seeds, sesame seeds and chopped nuts to cereals will boost their nutrient content. For young children you can grind the nuts into a fine powder.

3. Dairy Produce and Eggs
Give milk, yogurt or cheese to make sure your child gets the calcium he needs to build strong bones. Plain yogurt mixed with honey and fresh fruit is better than flavoured yogurts which tend to have a lot of added sugar. Choose whole milk rather than low-fat varieties unless your child is overweight. Eggs are an excellent source of protein and iron for your child. Try to give them at least two to three times a week.

Your child might like something from last night's dinner for breakfast, so be inventive with your leftovers. Foods like pizza, baked beans or Spanish omelette for breakfast are fine.

The Better Breakfast Plan

Use this plan as a guide to help you choose a healthy breakfast for your child every day.

MONDAY
- Fruity Swiss-Style Muesli (see page 12) or cereal topped with fruit
- Poached or fried egg with fingers of toast
- Glass of milk or orange juice

TUESDAY
- Plain yogurt with fresh berries topped with crunchy granola cereal
- Thinly sliced cheese or miniature cheeses
- Glass of orange juice

WEDNESDAY
- Boiled egg with fingers of toast
- Dried Fruit Compote (see page 16) or Fruit Salad with Honey Yogurt Dressing (see page 17)
- Glass of milk or hot chocolate

THURSDAY
- Cheese on toast, or Puffy Cheese Toasties (see page 152)
- Fresh fruit salad
- Milkshake, hot chocolate or fresh orange juice

FRIDAY
- Scrambled egg or omelette plain or filled
- Toast with peanut butter, Marmite or jam
- Fresh fruit
- Glass of milk

SATURDAY
- Porridge with honey, jam or stewed fruit
- Apple and All Bran Breakfast Muffin (see page 13)
- Fruity milkshake, milk or orange juice

SUNDAY
- Flipping Good Pancakes (see page 170) or waffles with fresh fruit
- Plain yogurt and honey
- Fresh orange juice

Fruity Swiss-style Muesli

Not suitable for freezing
SERVES 2
50 g (2 oz) muesli base, oatflakes or
   porridge oats
50 ml (2 fl oz) apple juice
120 ml (4 fl oz) natural yogurt
5 ml (1 tsp) honey
10 ml (2 tsp) fresh orange juice
1 small apple, peeled, grated or
   chopped assorted fruits in season
   eg: strawberries, kiwi, grapes,
   clementines

This healthy, delicious cereal makes a welcome alternative to the sugary over-processed cereals designed for children nowadays. It was invented by the famous Swiss physician, Dr Bircher-Benner to give his patients a healthy well-rounded breakfast. The traditional muesli uses cream, but I have used yogurt instead. You can add lots of different fruits like mango, peaches and plums and you could also use dried fruits like chopped dried apricots or raisins. I have used a muesli base made with wheat, barley and rye flakes, porridge oats and jumbo oats which I buy in my local health-food store. If you can't find this, then you could use plain oatflakes or porridge oats instead. This muesli can also be blended to a fine purée for babies.

Soak the muesli base or oats overnight in the apple juice. In the morning, mix with the rest of the ingredients and serve.

Apple and All Bran Breakfast Muffins

If you have no time to eat breakfast, then grab one of these and eat it on your way to school or to work. They're packed chock-full of delicious healthy ingredients. These will keep fresh in a sealed container for about 5 days.

Mix together the eggs, treacle, honey and oil and stir in the cereal, chopped apple and the raisins. Sift together the flour, baking soda, cinnamon and ginger and fold the dry ingredients into the egg mixture until just mixed. Finally fold in the chopped nuts (if using).

Line a muffin tray with paper cases and divide the mixture among them. Bake in an oven preheated to 200°C/400°F/Gas 6 for 20 minutes.

Suitable for freezing
MAKES 12 MUFFINS
2 eggs, lightly beaten
30 ml (2 tbsp) black treacle
50 ml (2 fl oz) runny honey
120 ml (4 fl oz) vegetable oil
85 g (3¼ oz) All Bran cereal
175g (6 oz) chopped,
    peeled apple
50 g (2 oz) raisins
125g (4½ oz) plain flour
10 ml (2 tsp) baking soda
2.5 ml (½ tsp) cinnamon
2.5 ml (½ tsp) ground ginger
25 g (1 oz) chopped pecans
    or walnuts (optional)

Strawberry and Banana Milkshake

Not suitable for freezing
MAKES 2 SMALL GLASSES
100 g (4 oz) strawberries, washed and hulled
1 small banana
120 ml (4 fl oz) milk

If the strawberries are not sweet, you may need to add a little sugar or honey to this milkshake.

Simply process all the ingredients in a blender.

Breakfast in a Glass

A friend of ours has a son called Joseph and he likes to whizz up his own fruity breakfast drinks in the morning. This is based on one of his concoctions and it's tasty and quick to make. You can create your own combinations using other fruits like mangoes or blueberries. Combine it with some toast or cereal for a nutritious breakfast.

Not suitable for freezing
MAKES 2 SMALL GLASSES
2 canned peach halves or 1 fresh
   juicy peach
1 banana
50 ml (2 fl oz) plain yogurt
50 ml (2 fl oz) orange juice
5 ml (1 tsp) honey

Process all the ingredients in a blender.

VARIATION

It's fun to serve drinks or milkshakes with fruity ice cubes. Simply put a small piece of fruit, like a halved grape or slice of strawberry, in each cube of an ice-cube tray, then fill with cold water and freeze. Press out the cubes of ice with the frozen fruit sealed inside when needed.

Dried Fruit Compote

Suitable for freezing
SERVES 4
1 X 250g (9 oz) packet mixed dried
  fruits (apple, apricot, prune, peach
  and pear)
425 ml (16 fl oz) mango or mango
  and apple naturally flavoured
  herbal tea

Dried fruits are one of nature's great health foods. They are a concentrated source of nutrients like iron and potassium and are also a good source of fibre. A bowl of dried fruit either by itself or with some plain yoghurt and crunchy breakfast cereal on top makes a delicious breakfast. Fruit flavoured herbal teas are available in health stores and some supermarkets. If you can't find mango tea then use unsweetened apple juice.

Put the dried fruit in a saucepan, pour over the tea, bring to the boil and then simmer for about 15 minutes or until the fruit is tender. Add some fresh fruit like sliced banana or strawberries before serving if you wish.

Fruit Salad with Honey Yogurt Dressing

Make up your own breakfast salad bowls with different combinations of fruits depending on which fruits are in season.

———————

Stir the yogurt into the honey. Mix the fruit together and spoon into a bowl. Top with the honey yogurt dressing.

Not suitable for freezing
SERVES 1
60 ml (4 tbsp) Greek yogurt
7.5 ml (1½ tsp) honey
1 apple, cored and cut into chunks
½ ripe mango, cubed
4 strawberries, quartered

Fruitfull Mornings

Not suitable for freezing

SERVES 1

FRUITY DIP

Pour a fruit yogurt, or fruit-flavoured fromage frais (raspberry is good) into a small serving bowl. Cut a variety of fruits like kiwi, strawberries, apples, bananas or pineapple into small pieces and arrange them on a plate around the yogurt dip.

SERVES 1

TRAFFIC LIGHT FRUIT SALAD

This salad has fresh raspberries or strawberries, juicy orange mango and green sliced kiwi fruit. Say Ready Steady Go and tuck in!

Arrange some sliced kiwi fruit around the sides of a glass or glass bowl and layer the rest at the bottom of the glass. Arrange the cubed mango on top and finish with a layer of sliced strawberries.

SERVES 1

STEWED FRUIT

Stewed fruit like cooking apple with a little brown sugar and cinnamon, or rhubarb with fresh orange juice and brown sugar, on its own or mixed with apple, makes a nice change for breakfast and can be prepared a day or two before.

SOUPA DOUPA

Real Chicken Stock

Suitable for freezing

MAKES 1.75 LITRES (3 PINTS)

1 large boiling chicken cut into
    quarters, plus giblets, or the
    carcass of a cooked roast
    chicken plus giblets
1 veal knuckle (optional)
2.25 litres (4 pints) water
2 large onions, roughly chopped
3 large carrots, roughly chopped
2 leeks, white part only, sliced
1 large parsnip, peeled and
    roughly chopped
½ celery stick with some leaves
1 sprig parsley or dried parsley
1 bay leaf
10 ml (2 tsp) tomato purée
2 chicken stock cubes, crumbled
    (optional – not suitable for very
    young children)
a little freshly ground black pepper

For maximum flavour, make chicken stock from a boiling chicken with its giblets. Ask your butcher to order one for you if he doesn't usually have them. The chicken joints can be lifted out when tender (after about 2 hours), the flesh removed and reserved for later use, and the chicken bones returned to the pan for a further 1½ to 2 hours. Otherwise, use the cooked carcass from a roast chicken with as many giblets as possible. These can be stockpiled in the freezer when cooking a roast chicken or making a chicken casserole. I like to add a veal knuckle to the stock as it improves the flavour, so ask your butcher to keep one for you.

Wash the chicken joints, veal knuckle and giblets, or break up the carcass if you are using this instead of a boiling chicken. Put in a large pan and cover with the water. Bring to the boil slowly and with a flat metal spoon, remove any scum from the surface. Add all the remaining ingredients and simmer very gently for 3½ to 4 hours, either in the oven at 150°C/300°F/Gas 2 or on top of the stove. If you are using a boiling chicken, strip the flesh from the bones after 2 hours. Set aside for use in other recipes and return the bones to the pan.

Allow to cool and refrigerate overnight. In the morning, you will be able to remove the layer of fat that settles on the surface. Strain the stock and discard the vegetables and bones. Ideally, make this in large batches and freeze it in 300 ml (½ pint) containers.

Vegetable Stock

To make vegetable stock, roughly chop the onion, carrot and leek, and sauté in the butter or margarine, for 10 minutes. Add the parsley, bay leaf, a few peppercorns and maybe a few extra vegetables or trimmings such as mushrooms, cabbage or celery. Pour over the cold water, bring to the boil, skim, reduce heat and simmer for about 45 minutes. Strain through a fine sieve, pressing on the vegetables with the back of a spoon to extract their juices. Bring the stock back to the boil and reduce to get a better flavour. Allow to cool, refrigerate and remove any fat from the surface.

Suitable for freezing
MAKES 900 ML (1½ PINTS)
1 large onion
1 carrot
1 leek
25 g (1oz) butter or margarine
1 sprig of parsley
1 bay leaf
peppercorns
extra vegetables
1.5 litres (2½ pints) water

Good and Healthy Lentil Soup

Suitable for freezing
SERVES 8
2 small onions, chopped
225 g (8 oz) carrots, chopped
50 g (2 oz) celery, finely sliced
25 g (1 oz) butter
100 g (4 oz) red lentils
1 medium potato (about 150 g/
   5 oz), diced
1.75 litres (3 pints) vegetable or
   chicken stock (see page 20 or 21)
salt and pepper

Lentils are not generally very popular with children but here's a very tasty way to enjoy them. This nutritious soup has proved very popular with my young team of tasters who never hesitate to give something the thumbs down if it doesn't appeal.

In a large saucepan, sauté the onions, carrot and celery gently in the butter for about 10 minutes or until softened. Add the lentils and diced potato, pour over the stock, stir and bring to the boil. Season with a little salt and pepper, cover with a lid and simmer gently for 45 to 50 minutes or until the lentils are soft. Purée in a blender. If you wish, you can stir a little cream into the soup and sprinkle with a few snipped chives.

Carrot Vichyssoise

When I was writing my first book, *The Complete Baby and Toddler Meal Planner*, my husband would get a different soup for dinner every night. What he didn't know was that they were, in fact, baby purées converted into soups by adding extra stock. Luckily he never complained because he loves soup and it goes to prove that you can cook for the whole family together even when your baby is only six months old! This soup has a lovely creamy texture and was one of my husband's and my baby's favourites! By adding only 450 ml (¾ pint) of stock and leaving out any seasonings this will make a very tasty purée for a baby.

Suitable for freezing
SERVES 4
25 g (1 oz) butter
½ onion, finely chopped
1 leek, carefully washed and sliced
1 large potato (275 g/10 oz), chopped
275 g (10 oz) carrots, sliced
1 litre (1¾ pints) chicken stock (see page 20)

Melt the butter and sauté the onion and leek until softened (about 6 minutes). Add the potato and carrots and pour in the stock. Bring to the boil and simmer for 20 to 25 minutes or until the vegetables are tender. Purée in a blender.

Tomato Soup with Hidden Vegetables and Rice

Suitable for freezing
SERVES 8

1 medium onion, chopped

1 medium carrot, grated (50–75 g/ 2–3 oz)

25 g (1 oz) butter

350 g (12 oz) tomatoes, skinned, deseeded and chopped

1 X 400 g (14 oz) can chopped tomatoes

750 ml (1¼ pints) chicken or vegetable stock (see page 20 or 21)

5 ml (1 tsp) sugar

40 g (1½ oz) long-grain rice

15 ml (1 tbsp) fresh basil, chopped (optional)

salt and pepper

A dding grated carrot to this soup brings out the sweet flavour of the tomatoes.

Sauté the onion and carrot in the butter until soft (about 6 minutes). Add the fresh and canned tomatoes and pour all the vegetables into a blender and purée. Return to a large saucepan. Add the stock, sugar, rice and basil and season lightly. Bring to the boil and simmer for 15 to 20 minutes or until the rice is cooked.

Spring Vegetable Soup with Alphabet Pasta

This is a great favourite with my family. My children like to play hunt the baked bean, seeing who can find the most baked beans in their bowl of soup. If you can't find tiny alphabet pasta, then substitute with the little star shapes that are used for soup pasta.

Sauté the onions in the olive oil for about 10 minutes in a large saucepan, stirring occasionally. Add the carrots, celery, potato, cabbage and French beans and sauté for 2 minutes. Pour in the chopped tomatoes and stock, bring to the boil, then cover and simmer for 25 to 30 minutes until the vegetables are tender. Add the baked beans and pasta about 10 minutes before the end of the cooking time. Season with a little salt and pepper to taste.

Suitable for freezing
SERVES 6
2 medium onions, finely chopped
45 ml (3 tbsp) olive oil
2 medium carrots, diced
2 sticks celery, trimmed and finely sliced
3 medium potatoes, diced
175 g (6 oz) shredded white cabbage
100 g (4 oz) French beans, topped and tailed and cut into 4 cm (1½") lengths
1 X 400 g (14 oz) can chopped tomatoes
2 litres (3½ pints) chicken or vegetable stock (see page 20 or 21)
1 X 205 g (7 oz) can baked beans
75 g (3 oz) tiny alphabet pasta
salt and freshly ground black pepper

Coming!
..Ready or not!

25

Lazy Day No-Fat Vegetable Soup

Suitable for freezing
SERVES 6
225 g (8 oz) swede, chopped
350 g (12 oz) carrots, chopped
2 leeks, trimmed and sliced
100 g (4 oz) potatoes, diced
900 ml (1½ pints) chicken or
    vegetable stock (see page 20 or 21)
300 ml (½ pint) milk

A lovely and very easy-to-make soup which is popular with children because of the sweet taste of the carrots and swede.

Put all the vegetables into a large saucepan, pour in the stock and bring to the boil. Cover and simmer for 30 minutes or until the vegetables are tender. Purée in a blender or food processor and stir in the milk. Return to the pan and reheat as necessary but do not boil. Season to taste.

Tasty Tomato Soup with Leeks

A creamy textured vegetable soup which can be a meal in itself served with salad, crusty bread and cheese.

Thoroughly wash the leeks and shred finely. Melt the butter in a large heavy-bottomed saucepan and sauté gently until softened but not brown. Add the tomatoes to the leeks, season lightly and add the sugar. Cover and simmer until the tomatoes are soft (about 5 minutes). Add the potato, pour in the stock and simmer gently for about 30 minutes or until the potato is soft. Blend in an electric blender to make a smooth soup.

Suitable for freezing
SERVES 5
3 leeks
25 g (1 oz) butter
450 g (1 lb) tomatoes, peeled, cut in quarters and deseeded
a little salt and pepper
5 ml (1 tsp) caster sugar
225 g (½ lb) potatoes, diced
900 ml (1½ pints) chicken stock (see page 20)

Warming Watercress Soup

Suitable for freezing
SERVES 5
1 large bunch of watercress
2 large leeks, white part only,
    finely sliced
25 g (1 oz) butter
1 large potato (225–275 g/
    8–10 oz), diced
600 ml (1 pint) chicken stock (see
    page 20)
300 ml (½ pint) milk
salt and freshly ground black pepper

Watercress leaves are among the healthiest of fresh salad vegetables, it is an excellent source of Vitamin C and betacarotene and adds a distinctive flavour to this creamy soup.

Thoroughly wash the watercress and remove the coarse stalks. Sauté the leeks in butter until softened (about 6 minutes), add the diced potato and watercress and toss in the butter for a couple of minutes. Pour in the stock and the milk, bring to the boil; then cover and simmer for about 30 minutes. Liquidise the soup in a blender, food processor or mouli (for a very smooth soup) and season to taste.

Lettuce, Leek and Pea Soup

Frozen peas can be just as nutritious as fresh peas because they are frozen very soon after they are picked so that all the vitamins are locked in. You could flavour this soup with a little freshly chopped mint if you like. Serving this soup could be the answer to getting your child to enjoy eating his greens!

Sauté the leeks in butter until soft (about 5 minutes). Add the lettuce and cook until the lettuce has wilted. Stir in the flour, cook for 1 minute and then add the sugar, peas and stock. Simmer until the peas are very soft (about 15 minutes or 4 to 5 minutes if frozen). Liquidise in a blender, adding more stock if the soup is too thick. Season to taste and stir in the cream.

Suitable for freezing
SERVES 6
3 leeks, white part only, finely sliced
40 g (1½ oz) butter
½ an iceberg lettuce, shredded
30 ml (2 tbsp) flour
5 ml (1 tsp) sugar
675 g (1½ lb) fresh peas or 450 g
   (1 lb) frozen peas
600 ml (1 pint) chicken stock (see
   page 20)
salt and pepper
120 ml (4 fl oz) single cream

Spiced Pumpkin or Butternut Squash Soup

Suitable for freezing
SERVES 6
1 onion, finely chopped
25 g (1 oz) butter
450 g (1 lb) peeled and chopped
   pumpkin or butternut squash or
   1 X 495 g (17½ oz) can puréed
   pumpkin
900 ml (1½ pints) chicken or
   vegetable stock (see page
   20 or 21)
1 bay leaf
pinch of nutmeg
2.5 cm (1 inch) fresh root ginger,
   peeled and grated or 2.5 ml (½ tsp)
   ground ginger (optional)
75 ml (3 fl oz) cream
salt and freshly ground black pepper
snipped chives for garnish (optional)

Vegetables like pumpkin and butternut squash are very popular in America but are not used so much in this country. However, recently I have noticed that they are becoming more readily available in supermarkets. These vegetables make wonderful soups and are very rich in betacarotene, the vegetable source of Vitamin A. As a short cut you can get excellent results using a can of puréed pumpkin.

_____

Sauté the onion in butter for about 8 minutes or until softened. Add the pumpkin and cook for 2 to 3 minutes. Pour in the stock and bring to the boil. Add the bay leaf and nutmeg and cover and simmer for 20 to 25 minutes or until the pumpkin is tender. Remove the bay leaf and purée in a blender or food processor and pour back into the pan. Over a gentle heat, stir in the ginger and cream and season lightly. Garnish with snipped chives if you wish.

Italian-Style Red Pepper and Courgette Soup

An unusual combination but the two flavours blend well together. I like to use small-sized courgettes for this soup as they have a sweeter flavour.

Sauté the shallots, garlic (if using) and red pepper in olive oil for about 10 minutes or until softened. Add the courgettes and cook for 1 minute. Pour in the chicken stock and cover and simmer for 20 minutes. Liquidise the soup in a blender or food processor and stir in the milk. Return to the pan to reheat as necessary. Season to taste and add the fresh basil.

Suitable for freezing
SERVES 4

2 large shallots, finely chopped

1 small clove of garlic (optional)

1 large red pepper, cored, deseeded and chopped (about 225 g/8 oz)

22.5 ml (1½ tbsp) olive oil

450 g (1 lb) small courgettes, topped and tailed and sliced into rounds

450 ml (¾ pint) chicken or vegetable stock (see page 20 or 21)

150 ml (¼ pint) milk

salt and pepper to taste

15 ml (1 tbsp) chopped fresh basil

Already Ready Soup

Suitable for freezing

SERVES 6

1 large onion, finely chopped

350 g (12 oz) potatoes diced

40 g (1½ oz) butter

350 g (12 oz) frozen mixed country
    vegetables (green beans, carrots,
    sweetcorn and peas)

600 ml (1 pint) chicken or vegetable
    stock (see page 20 or 21)

300 ml (½ pint) milk

50 g (2 oz) cooked rice

Frozen vegetables can be just as nutritious as fresh and in some circumstances, more so. For example, fresh green beans that are 3 days old have only got 50 per cent of their Vitamin C content, whereas frozen beans have no measurable loss of Vitamin C. So using a packet of ready-prepared frozen mixed vegetables as the basis for this soup is a handy short cut.

Sauté the onion and potato in the butter for 3 to 4 minutes. Add the frozen mixed vegetables and the stock, bring to the boil, then reduce the heat, cover and simmer for 20 minutes. Purée in a blender or food processor, add the milk and the cooked rice, heat through and season to taste.

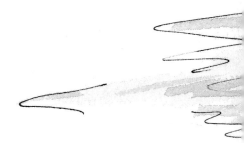

FISH FOR
THE FAMILY

Baked Fish with Tomatoes

Suitable for freezing
SERVES 4
450 g (1 lb) white fish (haddock,
    cod or halibut) skinned and filleted
seasoned flour
25 g (1 oz) butter
1 large onion, finely chopped
1 clove garlic, chopped (optional)
30–45 ml (2–3 tbsp) chopped
    fresh parsley
22.5 ml (1½ tbsp) vegetable oil
350 g (12 oz) tomatoes, skinned,
    deseeded and chopped
120 ml (4 fl oz) fish or chicken stock
    (see page 20)
30 ml (2 tbsp) white wine (optional)
30 ml (2 tbsp) toasted breadcrumbs

This is a quick and easy dish to make but is always popular. You could add chopped peppers or even stoned olives to the tomato sauce if you like. This is good served with creamy mashed potatoes or rice.

TO MAKE FISH STOCK, rinse fish bones and trimmings and simmer in lightly salted water for 30 minutes with chopped carrot, onion, celery, bay leaf, peppercorns, parsley, thyme and lemon rind and juice. Strain before using.

Cut the fish into four portions and coat with the seasoned flour. Sauté in the butter for 1 minute each side. Sauté the onion, garlic (if using) and parsley in vegetable oil until softened. Add the chopped tomatoes and sauté for 3 to 4 minutes. Pour in the chicken stock and wine (if using), bring to the boil, then reduce heat and simmer for another few minutes. Lay the fish in an ovenproof dish, cover with the sauce and sprinkle with the breadcrumbs. Cook, covered for about 20 minutes at 180°C/350°F/Gas 4.

Oven-Baked Fish with Ratatouille

This tasty topping turns a simple fillet of fish into something special.

___

Prepare the aubergine ahead of time by sprinkling with some salt and leaving for about 30 minutes in a colander with a small plate on top and a heavy weight on top of that. This will allow the bitter juices to drain away. Rinse off the salt and dry with kitchen paper. Sauté the chopped aubergine, onion and green pepper in the butter for 6 to 7 minutes, then stir in the chopped tomatoes and continue to cook for 2 to 3 minutes. Season with a little salt and pepper and mix in the oregano. Toss the breadcrumbs in a little butter. Season the fish and arrange in a well-buttered ovenproof dish and spread the vegetables over the fish. Scatter the breadcrumbs over the top and cover with foil. Bake in an oven preheated to 180°C/350°F/Gas 4 for 20 to 25 minutes.

Suitable for freezing
SERVES 2
75 g (3 oz) aubergine, peeled and chopped
salt and pepper
½ small onion, diced
25 g (1 oz) green pepper, cored, deseeded and diced
25 g (1 oz) butter
2 medium tomatoes, peeled, deseeded and chopped
1.25 ml (¼ tsp) oregano
30 ml (2 tbsp) breadcrumbs
a knob of butter
2 X 225 g (8 oz) fillets of haddock, cod or hake

Fish Fillets with a Cheese and Tomato Topping

Suitable for freezing
SERVES 4
2 medium sole or plaice, filleted and
    skinned (8 fillets)
a little salt and pepper
a knob of butter
30 ml (2 tbsp) lemon juice

CHEESE SAUCE
25 g (1 oz) butter
25 g (1 oz) flour
400 ml (14 fl oz) milk
75g (3 oz) grated Gruyère or
    Cheddar cheese
2 medium tomatoes, skinned and
    sliced

To turn this very tasty and appealing recipe into something special, pipe mashed potato all around the edge of the serving dish. It's easy to do using a plastic piping bag and large nozzle, then brush with beaten egg and place under the grill.

Place the fish in a greased microwave dish, season lightly, dot with butter and pour over the lemon juice. Cover (leaving an air vent) and cook on high for 3 minutes or until the fish flakes easily with a fork. Alternatively you can poach the fish fillets. To prepare the cheese sauce, melt the butter in a saucepan, stir in the flour and cook for 1 minute. Remove from the heat and gradually whisk in the milk, making sure that no lumps form. Return to the heat and bring to the boil, stirring constantly. Turn off the heat and stir in 65 g (2½ oz) of the cheese and season to taste. Place the fish fillets in a greased ovenproof dish and cover with the cheese sauce. Lay the slices of tomato on top and sprinkle with the remaining grated cheese. Place under a preheated grill until the topping is golden.

Baked Fish Gratin with Courgettes and Tomatoes

A n easy recipe to turn tender fillets of white fish into a tasty meal. This is good served with mashed potato or chips.

Coat the fish in seasoned flour and sauté in a mixture of butter and vegetable oil until lightly golden. Sauté the onion in the olive oil until softened, add the tomato purée and cook for 1 minute over a low heat. Add the chopped tomatoes and cook for 3 to 4 minutes, then stir in the sliced courgettes. Season and sprinkle with the oregano. Simmer for about 6 minutes or until the courgettes are tender. Lay the fish fillets in an ovenproof dish, spoon the tomato and courgette sauce over and scatter the cheese over the top. Bake in an oven preheated to 180°C/350°F/Gas 4 for 10 to 12 minutes and then finish off by placing under a grill for a few minutes until the cheese topping is bubbly and golden.

Suitable for freezing
SERVES 4

4 X 175 g (6 oz) fillets of cod or
   haddock, skinned
seasoned flour
15 g (½ oz) butter
15 ml (1 tbsp) vegetable oil
1 onion, chopped
15 ml (1 tbsp) olive oil
30 ml (2 tbsp) tomato purée
6 medium tomatoes, skinned,
   deseeded and roughly chopped
2 medium courgettes, topped and
   tailed and sliced
salt and freshly ground black pepper
2.5 ml (½ tsp) dried oregano
75 g (3 oz) grated Cheddar cheese

Fish Fillets with Cornflake and Cheese Topping

Suitable for freezing
SERVES 2
25 g (1 oz) each of carrot, leek and
    courgette, cut into matchsticks
25 g (1 oz) butter
5 ml (1 tsp) soy sauce
juice of 1 small orange
225 g (8 oz) fillet of cod or other
    white fleshy fish
salt and pepper
25 oz (1 oz) cornflakes, lightly
    crushed
25 g (1 oz) Cheddar cheese, grated

This combination of flavours works well even though it may seem rather unusual. If your child prefers, this can also be prepared without the vegetables. Simply mix together the melted butter, soy sauce and orange juice, pour this over the fish, add the topping and cook in the microwave for 4 minutes.

Sauté the vegetables in the butter until softened (about 4 minutes), add the soy sauce and orange juice and simmer for 1 minute. Season the fish and place in a greased microwave dish. Spoon over the vegetables and sauce. Mix together the crushed cornflakes and grated cheese and scatter this topping over the fish. Cook on High in a microwave for 4 to 5 minutes, covered but with an air vent. Alternatively, cook in a conventional oven at 180°C/350°F/Gas 4 for 20–25 minutes.

Very Easy Florentine Fillets

F illets of tender white fish on a bed of fresh spinach covered with cheese sauce is a classic and favourite combination. I buy microwave-in-the-bag spinach at my local supermarket which needs no preparation and takes 3 minutes to cook. The cheese sauce is very easy to prepare and the whole dish can be made in 10 minutes.

Microwave the spinach on High for 3 minutes or cook it in a saucepan with just a little water clinging to the leaves until wilted. Squeeze out excess moisture. Melt half the butter and sauté the spinach for 1 minute. Meanwhile, put the double cream, remaining butter and Parmesan in a small saucepan and heat gently until the butter has melted. Lightly season the fish and either sauté, microwave or poach until the fish flakes easily with a fork. Arrange the spinach on a greased ovenproof dish and place the fish fillet(s) on top. Pour the sauce over and sprinkle with the grated cheese. Brown under a preheated grill for 2 to 3 minutes.

Suitable for freezing
SERVES 2
225 g (8 oz) fresh spinach or
    100 g (4 oz) frozen
25 g (1 oz) butter
50 ml (2 fl oz) double cream
15 g (½ oz) grated Parmesan
1 X 225 g (8 oz) fillet of cod,
    haddock or 1 large sole or plaice,
    filleted and skinned
salt and pepper
30 ml (2 tbsp) grated Gruyère
    or Cheddar cheese

Salmon Parcels with Matchstick Vegetables

Not suitable for freezing
SERVES 2
1 carrot
½ leek, white part only
1 courgette
25 g (1 oz) butter
60 ml (4 tbsp) single cream
60 ml (4 tbsp) white wine
salt and pepper
2 large salmon steaks
2 sprigs of dill (optional)

Cooking fish in a parcel is simple and quick and seals in the flavour. When cooking in a parcel choose fish steaks rather than fillets of fish. There are many variations, for example: sautéed chopped onion, tomato and sweet pepper moistened with a little chicken stock would go well with cod steaks in a parcel.

Cut the carrot, leek and courgette into matchsticks and gently sauté in the butter for about 5 minutes. Stir in the wine, bring to the boil, then remove from the heat and stir in the cream. Season to taste. Cut two squares of silver foil, each large enough to enclose a salmon steak. Brush over the foil squares with melted butter and place a salmon steak on each piece of foil. Add the dill if using. Divide the vegetable mixture between them, fold over the foil and seal the edges. Taking care not to tear them, place the parcels on a baking sheet and bake in an oven preheated to 200°C/400°F/Gas 6 for 15 to 20 minutes. Alternatively, the parcels can be made using greaseproof paper and then the fish can be cooked in the microwave.

Little Parcels of Salmon on a Bed of Potatoes and Leek

The beauty of this recipe is that everything is sliced very thin. I ask my fishmonger to slice the salmon very thin and I cut the potatoes into very thin slices either by hand or in a food processor. Once the potatoes and leeks have been sautéed, it takes just 2 minutes to cook this in a microwave.

Melt the butter and sauté the potatoes and leek until lightly golden and tender. Cut two circles out of greaseproof paper large enough to make parcels around the fish and divide the potato and leek mixture between them. Season the salmon with a little salt and pepper and place the slices of salmon over the cooked vegetables. Pour 30 ml (2 tbsp) stock over each of the salmon fillets, dot with a little butter, add a sprig of dill, if you have one, and fold the paper over, sealing the edges to form two parcels. Place the parcels in the microwave and cook on full power for 2 minutes or until the fish flakes easily. If you don't have a microwave, you can wrap the salmon and vegetables in foil and bake in an oven preheated to 190°C/375°F/Gas 5 for about 10 minutes.

Suitable for freezing
SERVES 2
25 g (1 oz) butter, plus extra to finish
2 medium potatoes (about 100 g (4 oz) each), thinly sliced
1 leek, carefully washed and sliced
175 g (6 oz) salmon, thinly sliced
salt and pepper
60 ml (4 tbsp) chicken, fish or vegetable stock (see page 20, 34 or 21)
2 sprigs of dill (optional)

Sleeping Salmon on a Bed of Vegetables

Not suitable for freezing
SERVES 2
2 X 150 g (5 oz) thick-cut salmon
    fillets
salt and pepper
100 g (4 oz) cooked fresh or
    canned sweetcorn
75 g (3 oz) French beans, cooked
    and cut into pieces
225 g (8 oz) sliced boiled potatoes
15 g (½ oz) butter
5 ml (1 tsp) lemon juice
5 ml (1 tsp) finely chopped onion
2 tomatoes, peeled and sliced
15 g (½ oz) grated Parmesan cheese

Now that salmon has become so much cheaper, I use it quite a lot as I find that children often prefer it to white fish. This recipe can also be cooked in the microwave in about 5 minutes once all the ingredients are assembled.

Season the salmon with a little salt and pepper. In a well-greased ovenproof dish, arrange a layer of sweetcorn, green beans and then potato slices, sprinkling each layer with a little salt and pepper. Melt the butter and stir in the lemon juice and onion. Brush the salmon fillets all over with the melted butter mixture and lay them over the sliced potatoes. Cover the salmon with the sliced tomatoes, pour over any remaining butter and sprinkle with the grated Parmesan cheese. Cover with foil and bake in an oven preheated to 180°C/350°F/Gas 4 for 30 minutes.

Annabel's Simply Super Salmon Teriyaki

My husband and I both love Japanese food and this is one of my favourite recipes. It's a great favourite with my children too! It's worth investing in a bottle of sake and mirin (a sweet Japanese cooking wine) as you will want to make this recipe over and over again. Serve with basmati rice.

Cut the salmon steaks in half lengthwise and remove the bone. Mix the ingredients for the marinade together and stir over a medium heat in a saucepan until the sugar has dissolved. Marinate the salmon in the sauce for 10 minutes. Heat half the oil and sauté the mushrooms for 2 minutes, then add the beansprouts and cook for 2 minutes more. Meanwhile, drain the salmon, reserving the marinade. Heat the remaining oil in a frying pan and sauté the salmon for 1 to 2 minutes on each side or until slightly browned. Be careful not to overcook the fish or it will become dry. Pour away the excess oil from the frying pan. Pour a little of the teriyaki sauce over the salmon and continue to cook for a few minutes, basting occasionally. Simmer the remaining teriyaki sauce until it thickens. Divide the vegetables among 4 plates, place the salmon on top and pour the teriyaki sauce over the top.

Not suitable for freezing
SERVES 4
2 salmon steaks complete with skin (about 400 g/14 oz) or 4 thick fillets of salmon
50 ml (2 fl oz) vegetable oil
100 g (4 oz) button mushrooms
100 g (4 oz) beansprouts

MARINADE
50 ml (2 fl oz) soy sauce
50 ml (2 fl oz) sake
25 ml (1 fl oz) mirin
15 g (½ oz) sugar

Salmon Fillets in a Watercress and Courgette Sauce

Not suitable for freezing
SERVES 4
450 g (1 lb) salmon fillets, skinned
salt and pepper
melted butter
lemon juice
50 g (2 oz) finely chopped shallot
25 g (1 oz) butter
150 g (5 fl oz) chicken stock or fish
   stock (see page 20 or 34)
175 g (6 oz) sliced courgettes
50 g (2 oz) watercress, leaves only
30–45 ml (2–3 tbsp) double
   cream

S almon has become much more plentiful and cheaper in recent years. This combination of salmon in a creamy watercress sauce works well. This is good served with mangetout and new potatoes.

Lightly season the salmon, brush with melted butter and squeeze over a little lemon juice. Cook on High in a microwave for about 6 minutes or until the fish flakes easily with a fork. If you do not have a microwave, place each fillet on a piece of foil, lightly season, brush with melted butter, add a squeeze of lemon and wrap the foil so that there is room around the fish but the parcel is sealed. Bake in an oven preheated to 180°C/350°F/Gas 4 for 20 to 25 minutes or until the fish is cooked. Meanwhile, sauté the shallots for 2 minutes, add the courgettes and sauté for 2 to 3 minutes. Pour the chicken stock over the courgettes, bring to the boil, reduce the heat and cook for about 5 minutes. Add the watercress and continue to cook for 2 minutes. Remove from the heat. Purée in a blender, stir in the cream, season to taste and pour the sauce over the salmon fillets. Heat through before serving.

Tagliatelle with Fresh Salmon and Prawns

F or speed and simplicity I sometimes use a packet sauce and mix it with fresh ingredients to make a meal. Some sauces taste very synthetic and salty but I find that hollandaise sauce in a packet can really taste rather good.

Cook the pasta in plenty of lightly salted boiling water and set aside. Meanwhile, sauté the onion in the butter until softened. Cut the salmon into bite-sized pieces and sauté for 2 to 3 minutes. Add the peeled prawns, cooked frozen peas (if using) and the chopped tomato. Make up the hollandaise sauce according to the packet instructions. Mix the sauce with the salmon and prawn mixture. Pour this sauce over the cooked tagliatelle and sprinkle with dill if wished.

Not suitable for freezing
SERVES 4
225 g (8 oz) tagliatelle
½ onion, finely chopped
a knob of butter
225 g (8 oz) salmon
100 g (4 oz) cooked peeled prawns
40 g (1½ oz) frozen peas (optional)
2 tomatoes, skinned, deseeded and chopped
1 X 25 g packet Crosse and Blackwell Hollandaise sauce mix mixed with 40 g (1½ oz) butter and 300 ml (½ pint) milk
a little chopped fresh dill (optional)

Twiddly Tuna and Pasta Bake

Not suitable for freezing
SERVES 4

1 small onion, finely chopped
25 g (1 oz) butter
100 g (4 oz) mushrooms, sliced
15 ml (1 tbsp) chopped fresh parsley
15 ml (1 tbsp) flour
175 ml (6 fl oz) milk
1 X 295 g (10½ oz) can of
  condensed mushroom soup
100 g (4 oz) frozen peas
1 X 200 g (7 oz) can tuna in
  vegetable oil
225 g (8 oz) noodles, cooked and
  drained
50 g (2 oz) ready salted crisps
50 g (2 oz) grated Cheddar cheese

An easy dish to put together using store-cupboard ingredients. The crunchy topping made from crisps and grated cheese makes this dish particularly 'child friendly'.

Sauté the onion in the butter until softened, add the sliced mushrooms and parsley and cook for 2 minutes. Add the flour and mix well. Gradually stir in the milk, bring to the boil and simmer for 1 minute. Stir in the mushroom soup and heat through. Cook the peas until tender. Drain and flake the tuna and mix into the mushroom sauce. Pour the mushroom sauce over the cooked pasta and spoon the mixture into an ovenproof dish. Top with the crisps and grated cheese. Put under a hot grill for a few minutes until the cheese has melted and browned.

Souper Tagliatelle

Heinz tomato soup has long been a great favourite with children. Here I have combined it with tuna, button mushrooms, Cheddar cheese and tagliatelle for a simple but very tasty recipe.

———————

Cook the pasta in plenty of boiling salted water with a teaspoon of oil until just *al dente* and set aside. Meanwhile, sauté the onion in the butter until softened, add the sliced mushrooms and sauté for 2 to 3 minutes. Stir in the flour and cook for 30 seconds. Mix in the tomato soup, 120 ml (4 fl oz) water, season with the herbs and add a little freshly ground black pepper. Bring to the boil and simmer for about 5 minutes, stirring occasionally. Flake the tuna and stir into the sauce.

To make the cheese sauce, melt the butter in a saucepan, stir in the flour and cook over a gentle heat for 1 minute. Gradually whisk in the milk. Bring to the boil, then lower the heat and simmer for 2 to 3 minutes or until the sauce is smooth. Remove from the heat and stir in 75 g (3 oz) of the cheese.

Mix the tagliatelle with the tomato sauce and the flaked fish and arrange in a 25 X 20 X 8 cm (10 X 8 X 3 inches) ovenproof dish. Cover with the cheese sauce and sprinkle over the remaining cheese. Heat through and then place under a preheated grill for a few minutes until golden and bubbling.

Suitable for freezing
SERVES 5
225g (8 oz) green and white
    tagliatelle
1 onion, finely chopped
25 g (1 oz) butter
100 g (4 oz) button mushrooms,
    sliced
30 ml (2 tbsp) flour
1 X 405 g (14 oz) can Heinz
    cream of tomato soup
2.5 ml (½ tsp) Italian seasoning
freshly ground black pepper
1 X 400 g (14 oz) can tuna in oil,
    drained

CHEESE SAUCE
25 g (1 oz) butter
25 g (1 oz) flour
350 ml (12 fl oz) milk
1 ml (¼ tsp) dried mustard powder
100 g (4 oz) grated Cheddar
    cheese

Golden Knots of Plaice with Oven-Baked Chips

Suitable for freezing

MAKES ABOUT 12 KNOTS OF
    PLAICE

1 medium-sized plaice, filleted

1 egg, lightly beaten

15 ml (1 tbsp) milk

salt

65 g (2½ oz) dry white breadcrumbs

30 ml (2 tbsp) freshly grated
    Parmesan cheese

30–45 ml (2–3 tbsp) fresh herbs,
    finely chopped, eg: parsley

seasoned flour

oil for frying

OVEN-BAKED CHIPS

675 g (1½ lb) waxy potatoes

salt

45 ml (3 tbsp) vegetable oil or
    melted butter

pinch of dried thyme or mixed herbs
    (optional)

These knots of plaice can look very attractive. You may find some pieces of the fish too short to tie in a knot in which case just coat them with the breadcrumbs and make them into goujons. Serve with tartare sauce or tomato ketchup. These are good accompanied with homemade chips and my oven-baked version is much lower in fat than normal chips.

Cut the plaice into thin strips about 18 cm (7 inches) long and tie them in knots. Mix the beaten egg with the milk and a pinch of salt. Mix the breadcrumbs, Parmesan and herbs together. Dip the fish into the seasoned flour, then into the egg mixture and finally roll in the breadcrumbs. Deep fry or sauté in the oil until golden.

TO PREPARE THE CHIPS, peel the potatoes and cut into fairly thick chips. Put them in a large saucepan of lightly salted water, bring to the boil and boil for about 5 minutes. Drain the chips and dry on absorbent kitchen paper. Put the oil in a roasting tin and heat in the oven at 220°C/425°F/ Gas 7. Add the chips, turning them to make sure that they are coated with the oil and sprinkle with the herbs if using. Spread them out in a single layer and bake for about 35 minutes until the chips are crisp and golden.

Posh Fish
with Creamy Prawn Sauce

This delicious fish recipe is wonderful for dinner parties. It's the sort of fish dish you would expect to get at a posh restaurant and it's really simple to make!

Take 4 pieces of foil, brush the centre of each with a little melted butter. Season the fish fillets and lay each one on a piece of foil. Brush with the melted butter, sprinkle with the herbs and squeeze over some lemon juice. Wrap the foil loosely around the fish to make a sealed parcel and bake in an oven preheated to 180°C/350°F/Gas 4 for 20 to 25 minutes. Alternatively, wrap in greaseproof paper and cook in the microwave for 4 minutes.

TO PREPARE THE SAUCE, mix together the stock, wine, tomato purée and cream. Heat gently and mix a little of the sauce in a bowl together with the cornflour. Add this to the rest of the sauce and gently bring to the boil, stirring all the time until thickened. Add 175 g (6 oz) of the prawns and liquidise the sauce in a blender. Return to the pan. Season to taste, add the remaining prawns and heat through. Once the fish is cooked, drain away any cooking liquid and arrange each fillet on a plate. Pour over the sauce.

Not suitable for freezing
SERVES 4
40 g (1½ oz) butter
4 X 225 g (8 oz) fillets of fish,
    eg: cod, haddock, hake, sole
salt and pepper
15 ml (1 tbsp) chopped fresh dill or
    parsley
lemon juice
150 ml (¼ pint) fish or chicken stock
    (see page 34 or 20)
50 ml (2 fl oz) dry white wine
10 ml (2 tsp) tomato purée
120 ml (4 fl oz) double cream
15 ml (1 tbsp) cornflour
275 g (10 oz)
    cooked shelled
    prawns (fresh or
    frozen)

Fish and Chip Pie

Not suitable for freezing
SERVES 4
450 g (1 lb) potatoes, cut into small
    cubes
30 ml (2 tbsp) vegetable oil
1 X 25 g (1 oz) packet savoury
    white sauce mixed with 300 ml
    (½ pint) milk
300 ml (1 lb) skinned cod or
    haddock fillet, cut into chunks
25 g (1 oz) frozen peas
25 g (1 oz) frozen sweetcorn
25 g (1 oz) grated Gruyère or
    Cheddar cheese

Instead of the traditional mashed potato topping, I have used a crispy potato and cheese topping which I think appeals to children much more. If you like, you can add some cooked prawns to this pie or use other fish like salmon or smoked haddock.

———————

Sauté the potatoes in oil until golden brown and crispy (15 to 20 minutes). Meanwhile, make up the white sauce with the milk according to the packet instructions. Add the cubed fish and frozen vegetables to the sauce and simmer for about 10 minutes or until the fish is cooked. Spoon the fish into a suitable ovenproof dish and top with the sautéed potatoes. Sprinkle with the grated cheese and cook under a preheated grill for a few minutes.

Haddock with a Coat of Mushrooms

T he sautéed mushroom and onion and the breadcrumb mixture add a delicious flavour to these haddock fillets.

Lightly season the fish and arrange over the base of a greased ovenproof dish. Melt the butter in a frying pan, sauté the onion until softened, add the chopped mushrooms and sauté for about 3 minutes. Spread the mushroom mixture over the fish fillets. Mix together the breadcrumbs and cheeses and sprinkle over the fish. Bake in an oven preheated to 180°C/350°F/Gas 4 for about 25 minutes or until the fish flakes easily with a fork.

Suitable for freezing
SERVES 4
4 X 100 g (4 oz) haddock fillets
salt and pepper
25 g (1 oz) butter
1 large onion, finely chopped
175 g (6 oz) brown cap or button
   mushrooms, finely chopped
25 g (1 oz) fresh white breadcrumbs
40 g (1½ oz) Cheddar cheese,
   grated
15 ml (1 tbsp) freshly grated
   Parmesan

Keep It Simple

Not suitable for freezing
SERVES 4
2 medium Dover or lemon sole or
   plaice, skinned and filleted
   (8 fillets)
seasoned flour
50 g (2 oz) butter
10 ml (2 tsp) teaspoon chopped
   mixed herbs like chives and parsley
10 ml (2 tsp) fresh lemon juice

This quick and easy recipe for fillets of sole or plaice is very popular. Serve with the lemon and herb sauce and maybe some homemade chips sprinkled with vinegar and served in newspaper for a real treat!

Coat the fish fillets in seasoned flour. Heat a heavy frying pan and add half the butter, sauté the fish fillets until golden brown, this will only take a few minutes each side. Remove the fillets and arrange in a hot dish. Wipe out the frying pan, add the remaining butter. Allow to colour a delicate brown, then add the chopped herbs and lemon juice. Pour over the fish and serve immediately.

Just a little fishy on a little dishy

Trout à L'Orange

This simple recipe takes less than 10 minutes to prepare. I serve the fish whole and sprinkle with some flaked almonds, browned in a knob of butter for adults. For children, I remove the fillets from the bone once the trout is cooked and pour over some of the orange sauce. Be careful of the fish bones; if you prefer you can use fillets of trout rather than the whole fish.

Not suitable for freezing
SERVES 4

4 rainbow or salmon trout
60 ml (4 tbsp) seasoned flour
40 g (1½ oz) butter
30 ml (2 tbsp) vegetable oil
2 oranges
30 ml (2 tbsp) soy sauce

Coat the trout with the seasoned flour. Heat the butter and oil in a large frying pan, add the trout and fry on each side for 4 to 5 minutes until golden and cooked through. Remove the trout and keep warm. Stir the orange juice and soy sauce into the juices in the pan, bring to the boil and simmer for 1 to 2 minutes.

Lara's Tasty 10-Minute Prawn Stir-Fry

Not suitable for freezing
SERVES 3
15 ml (1 tbsp) vegetable oil
50 g (2 oz) courgettes cut into
    matchsticks or 50 g (2 oz)
    mangetout
50 g (2 oz) baby sweetcorn, cut in
    half
120 ml (4 fl oz) chicken stock
    (see page 20)
5 ml (1 tsp) light soy sauce
10 ml (2 tsp) sake (rice wine) or
    sherry
10 ml (2 tsp) cornflour
225 g (8 oz) cooked king prawns
50 g (2 oz) bamboo shoots
    (optional)

My daughter Lara loves prawns and this is a very quick and simple recipe that I make for her which she really likes. I buy fresh cooked king prawns in my local supermarket but if you can't find them use frozen prawns instead. Lara likes to eat this with Chinese Noodles and Beansprouts (see page 119).

Heat the oil in a wok or frying pan and sauté the courgette sticks or mangetout and sweetcorn for 1 to 2 minutes. Remove the vegetables and set aside. Mix together the chicken stock, soy sauce, sake and cornflour. Pour the mixture into the wok and stir constantly while bringing to the boil. Reduce the heat and simmer for 1 to 2 minutes until thickened. Stir in the prawns and bamboo shoots (if using) and heat through.

NICE AND EASY
POULTRY AND MEAT

'Risotto' with Tomatoes and Chicken

Suitable for freezing
SERVES 2
1 onion, finely chopped
½ red pepper, cored, deseeded and
    finely chopped
1 small garlic clove, crushed
    (optional)
15 ml (1 tbsp) fresh parsley, chopped
22.5 ml (1½ tbsp) vegetable oil
175 g (6 oz) long-grain rice
1 X 400 g (14 oz) can chopped
    tomatoes, drained
15 ml (1 tbsp) tomato purée
375 ml (12 fl oz) chicken stock
    (see page 20)
45 ml (3 tbsp) pure apple juice
2.5 ml (½ tsp) Worcestershire sauce
1 large breast of chicken, diced
salt and freshly ground black pepper

This tasty rice is very simple to prepare and you don't need to stand over the stove ladling in the stock little by little as you would for a true risotto. You can add 50 g (2 oz) frozen peas to the rice about 7 minutes before the end of the cooking time if you like. For vegetarians, you could leave out the chicken, use vegetable stock and maybe add some extra vegetables like diced carrots or courgettes.

Sauté the onion, red pepper, garlic (if using) and parsley in the oil for about 4 minutes. Wash and drain the rice and spoon it together with all the other ingredients except the chicken into a large saucepan. Bring to the boil, cover and simmer for 15 minutes. Add extra stock if necessary. Add the diced chicken and simmer stirring occasionally for 15 to 20 minutes or until the rice is tender and the chicken is cooked through. Season to taste.

Italian-Style Chicken with Mozzarella and Tomato

A good homemade tomato sauce is always popular and forms the basis of many recipes. Put together with thin slices of mozzarella, fresh basil and chicken breasts, it makes an irresistible combination.

TO MAKE THE TOMATO SAUCE, heat the oil in a frying pan and sauté the onion, celery, red pepper, parsley and garlic (if using) for about 5 minutes or until tender. Add the chopped tomatoes, tomato purée, stock, sugar and basil. Season to taste, bring to the boil and then simmer for 30 minutes, stirring occasionally.

Flatten the chicken with a rolling pin (it's a good idea to place the chicken breasts between two sheets of cling film for this) and coat the chicken breasts in seasoned flour. Sauté the chicken in the oil for about 3 minutes on each side – the chicken should look golden on the outside. In an ovenproof dish, spoon a layer of tomato sauce over the base. Lay the chicken on top, cover with slices of mozzarella and spoon the rest of the tomato sauce on top. Mix together the Parmesan and breadcrumbs and sprinkle these over the chicken. Bake in an oven preheated to 180°C/350°F/Gas 4 for 25 to 30 minutes.

Suitable for freezing
SERVES 4
4 chicken breasts
seasoned flour
45 ml (3 tbsp) vegetable oil
1 X 125 g (4½ oz) packet
    mozzarella cheese
45 ml (3 tbsp) freshly grated
    Parmesan cheese
30 ml (2 tbsp) breadcrumbs

TOMATO SAUCE
22.5 ml (1½ tbsp) olive oil
1 onion, finely chopped
1 stick celery, finely chopped
1 small red pepper, finely chopped
15 ml (1 tbsp) chopped fresh parsley
1 garlic clove, crushed (optional)
1 X 400 g (14 oz) can chopped
    tomatoes
15 ml (1 tbsp) tomato purée
150 ml (¼ pint) chicken stock (see
    page 20)
5 ml (1 tsp) caster sugar
15 ml (1 tbsp) fresh chopped basil
salt and freshly ground pepper

Chicken Baked in a Rich Tomato Sauce

Suitable for freezing
SERVES 4

4 chicken portions on the bone,
    remove any excess fat
25 g (1 oz) butter
15 ml (1 tbsp) olive oil
1 onion, finely chopped
1 clove garlic, crushed
30 ml (2 tbsp) plain flour
450 ml (15 fl oz) chicken stock (see
    page 20)
60 ml (4 tbsp) white wine
60 ml (4 tbsp) tomato purée
15 ml (1 tbsp) soy sauce
30 ml (2 tbsp) fresh chopped basil
2.5 ml (½ tsp) dried mixed herbs
black pepper
175 g (6 oz) button mushrooms,
    sliced

This tasty chicken is nice served with tagliatelle or rice. You can leave out the mushrooms if you prefer.

Sauté the chicken in the butter and oil until browned. Remove it with a slotted spoon and put it into a small casserole. Fry the onion and garlic until softened and golden. Stir in the flour and cook for a few seconds. Add the stock, wine, tomato purée, soy sauce, herbs and pepper. Bring to the boil then cook in an oven preheated to 160°C/325°F/Gas 3 for about 45 minutes. Twenty minutes before the end, add the sliced mushrooms.

Stuffed Breasts of Chicken in a Parcel

Cooking chicken breasts in foil keeps them lovely and tender and moist. The spinach and mushroom stuffing is simple to make and the whole dish is finished off with a wonderful fresh tomato sauce. This is a real treat for supper.

Melt the butter and sauté the shallots or onion until softened. Add the mushrooms and cook for 2 minutes. Drain and chop the spinach and add to the mushrooms and sauté for 1 minute. Season to taste.

Lightly season the chicken and with a sharp knife, cut a pocket in each of the chicken breasts and stuff with the spinach and mushrooms. Lay each breast of chicken on a piece of foil large enough to make a parcel, dot each breast of chicken with butter and add 15 ml (1 tbsp) of stock and 7.5 ml (½ tbsp) of wine. Fold over each piece of foil to make a loose but secure parcel and bake in an oven preheated to 200°C/400°F/Gas 6 for about 20 minutes or until the chicken is cooked through.

Meanwhile prepare the tomato sauce. First sauté the shallot in butter until softened. Add the tomatoes, sauté for 2 to 3 minutes, then add the chicken stock, wine and basil. Bring to the boil and simmer for about 8 minutes. Once the chicken breasts are cooked, pour the cooking juices into the sauce and heat through. Season to taste and pour some tomato sauce over each chicken breast.

Suitable for freezing

SERVES 4

25 g (1 oz) butter

2 shallots or ½ small onion, chopped

100 g (4 oz) button, brown cap or shiitake mushrooms, finely chopped

150 g (5 oz) frozen spinach or 275 g (10 oz) fresh spinach, cooked

salt and freshly ground black pepper

4 chicken breasts

15 g (½ oz) butter

60 ml (4 tbsp) chicken stock (see page 20)

30 ml (2 tbsp) white wine

FRESH TOMATO SAUCE

2 shallots or ½ onion, finely chopped

25 g (1 oz) butter

450 g (1 lb) plum tomatoes, skinned, deseeded and chopped

120 ml (4 fl oz) chicken stock (see page 20)

60 ml (4 tbsp) white wine

15 ml (1 tbsp) chopped fresh basil or 2.5 ml (½ tsp) dried basil

salt and pepper

Tender Chicken Breasts with Creamy Mushroom Sauce

Suitable for freezing
SERVES 4
50 g (2 oz) butter
4 chicken breasts
2 medium onions, finely sliced
1 garlic clove, crushed
30 ml (2 tbsp) chopped parsley
175 g (6 oz) button mushrooms,
    sliced
200 ml (7fl oz) milk
1 X 295 g (10 oz) can condensed
    mushroom soup
dash of sherry (optional)
salt and pepper

I use a can of Campbell's condensed mushroom soup to make this very tasty recipe and I serve the chicken breasts on a bed of rice or noodles.

Melt the butter and sauté the chicken breasts until slightly browned (they will be cooked again later). Remove from the pan with a slotted spoon and set aside. Add the onion, garlic and parsley to the pan and sauté for about 8 minutes or until softened. Add the mushrooms and sauté for 2 to 3 minutes. Add the milk, simmer for 1 minute, then add the soup and sherry (if using). Simmer for a few minutes, stirring occasionally and season to taste. Return the chicken to the pan, cover and cook over a gentle heat for 30 minutes or until the chicken is tender and cooked through.

Chicken in a Creamy Sauce with Summer Vegetables

Tender succulent pieces of chicken are quickly cooked with fresh vegetables in a creamy sauce flavoured with a little white wine and lemon juice. This is good served on a bed of rice. The alcohol in the wine evaporates during cooking but adds flavour to the dish.

———————

Cut the chicken into bite-sized pieces and sauté in half the oil and butter until just cooked. Meanwhile, steam, microwave or boil the carrots and beans separately until tender but still crisp. Remove the chicken from the pan and set aside. Add the rest of the butter and oil to the pan and sauté the shallots or onion until softened. Add the mushrooms and sauté for 2 minutes. Sprinkle with the flour and cook for 1 minute. Gradually add the wine and chicken stock, bring to the boil, stirring until thickened. Add the carrots and beans and simmer for 2 minutes. Mix in the cream and chicken and simmer for 5 minutes or until the chicken is cooked through. Stir in the lemon juice and season to taste.

Suitable for freezing
SERVES 4

4 chicken breasts
25 g (1 oz) butter
15 ml (1 tbsp) vegetable oil
75 g (3 oz) baby carrots, cut into strips
75 g (3 oz) French beans
3 shallots, or 1 medium onion, finely chopped
100 g (4 oz) button mushrooms, sliced
15 ml (1 tbsp) flour
50 ml (2 fl oz) dry white wine
250 ml (8 fl oz) chicken stock (see page 20)
45 to 60 ml (3 to 4 tbsp) double cream
22.5 ml (1½ tbsp) fresh lemon juice
salt and pepper

Chicken with a Touch of Class

Suitable for freezing
SERVES 4
1 large onion, sliced
30 ml (2 tbsp) fresh parsley, chopped
45 ml (3 tbsp) vegetable oil
4 small chicken breasts
2 tomatoes, skinned, deseeded
    and chopped (about 200 g/7 oz)
1 chicken stock cube, carefully
    crumbled
salt and pepper
15 ml (1 tbsp) flour
120 ml (4 fl oz) white wine
50 ml (2 fl oz) water
1 X 300 g (10½ oz) can button
    mushrooms

Dishes with wine aren't necessarily precluded from family meals with children since, as in the previous recipe, the alcohol content of wine evaporates during the cooking process. The wine adds a special flavour to this recipe which is popular with all my family, even Scarlett my four year old. I cut the chicken into pieces and serve on a bed of rice for the children's portions.

Sauté the onion and parsley in the vegetable oil for 3 to 4 minutes. Add the chicken breasts, tomatoes and crumbled stock cube. Season with freshly ground black pepper and cook for 5 minutes. Blend in the flour, then stir in the white wine and the water. Bring to the boil, then reduce the heat,, add the mushrooms, cover and cook for 30 minutes or until the chicken is cooked through.

Polka Dot Chicken

These bite-sized chunks of chicken with colourful diced vegetables in a light vinaigrette, are good served hot or cold. Serve on their own, on a bed of rice or with some small cooked pasta shapes.

Mix together the soy sauce, beaten egg white, sake or sherry and the cornflour and marinate the chicken for about 20 minutes. Heat the oil in a wok or frying pan and sauté the chicken for 3 minutes, add the spring onions and continue to sauté until the chicken is cooked through. Meanwhile, steam the pepper, courgette and sweetcorn seasoned with a little salt for 5 minutes. Mix together the cooked chicken and vegetables. To prepare the vinaigrette, whisk the vinegar together with the mustard and sugar, whisk in the oil and season to taste. Pour the vinaigrette over the chicken and mix well.

Not suitable for freezing

SERVES 2

15 ml (1 tbsp) soy sauce

1 lightly beaten egg white

15 ml (1 tbsp) sake (rice wine) or sherry

10 ml (2 tsp) cornflour

2 chicken breasts, cut into bite-sized chunks

30 ml (2 tbsp) vegetable oil

2 spring onions, finely sliced

½ small red pepper, diced

175 g (6 oz) diced courgette (unpeeled)

175 g (6 oz) frozen sweetcorn

salt

VINAIGRETTE

30 ml (2 tbsp) white wine vinegar

1.25 ml (¼ tsp) dry mustard powder

5 ml (1 tsp) sugar

60 ml (4 tbsp) olive oil

salt and pepper to taste

Coronation Chicken

Not suitable for freezing
SERVES 3
3 breasts of chicken on the bone
a sprig of parsley
bay leaf
½ small onion, peeled
250 ml (8 fl oz) chicken stock (see
    page 20)
½ small onion, finely chopped

CURRY SAUCE
20 g (¾ oz) butter
5 ml (1 tsp) mild curry powder
15 ml (1 tbsp) plain flour
45 ml (3 tbsp) mayonnaise
30 ml (2 tbsp) apricot jam or mango
    chutney (sieved)
squeeze of lemon juice

This chicken has a delicious creamy sweet and sour taste. Serve with rice.

Skin the chicken breasts and put into a saucepan together with the parsley, bay leaf and onion and pour the chicken stock over. Cover and simmer for about 20 minutes or until the chicken is thoroughly cooked. Remove the chicken and set aside, discard the onion and herbs but reserve the poaching liquid.

TO MAKE THE SAUCE, sauté the onion in butter until softened, stir in the curry powder and cook gently for a few minutes. Stir in the flour and then whisk in the poaching liquid. Simmer, stirring until the sauce thickens for about 5 minutes. Leave to cool, then stir in the mayonnaise, sieved apricot jam and the lemon juice. Take the chicken off the bone and cut into neat strips. Pour the sauce over and mix well.

Chicken in a Mild Curried Sauce with Butterfly Pasta

This has a lovely flavour. I have always liked the combination of apple and chicken. Add more curry powder if you like and you can substitute cooked rice for the pasta if you wish.

Sauté the onion and garlic (if using) in the oil until softened. Meanwhile cook the pasta according to the instructions on the packet and set aside. When the onion is cooked, stir in the curry powder, then add the chicken and sauté until cooked on the outside. Stir in the flour and the apple juice and simmer for 1 minute, stirring. Gradually add the chicken stock and simmer for 6 to 8 minutes or until the chicken is cooked through properly. Add the cooked frozen peas, chopped tomato and cooked pasta. Stir in the cream and heat through. Season to taste.

Suitable for freezing but cook the pasta fresh

SERVES 4

1 large onion or 2 small onions, finely sliced

1 clove garlic, crushed (optional)

45 ml (3 tbsp) vegetable oil

175 g (6 oz) butterfly pasta

10 ml (2 tsp) mild curry powder

2 chicken breasts, cut into small chunks

22.5 ml (1½ tbsp) flour

75 ml (3 fl oz) apple juice

350 ml (12 fl oz) chicken stock (see page 20)

50 g (2 oz) frozen peas, cooked

2 tomatoes, skinned, seeded and chopped

75 ml (3 fl oz) single cream

a little salt and pepper

Fruity Curried Chicken with Rice

Suitable for freezing
SERVES 2
2 chicken breasts on the bone
15 ml (1 tbsp) vegetable oil
15 g (½ oz) butter or margarine
1 small onion, finely sliced
1 apple, thinly sliced
15 ml (1 tbsp) flour
7.5–10 ml (1½–2 tsp) mild curry
  powder
350 ml (12 fl oz) chicken stock
  (see page 20)
15 ml (1 tbsp) tomato purée
15 ml (1 tbsp) lemon juice
15 ml (1 tbsp) mango chutney
15 ml (1 tbsp) sultanas
cooked basmati rice

For children this is a good introduction to curry as it's very mild and the fruit brings out a sweet taste which children like. For a quick meal you can also prepare this sauce with ready-cooked chicken, simply heat through and serve on a bed of basmati rice. It's fun to accompany this dish with poppadums which can be bought in packs ready prepared.

Trim the chicken breasts of excess fat or skin, sauté in the oil until golden but not cooked through and set aside. Melt the butter in a frying pan and gently sauté the sliced onion and apple until soft. Stir in the flour and curry powder and cook for 1 minute. Gradually stir in the stock. Add the tomato purée, lemon juice, mango chutney and sultanas. Bring to the boil and simmer for about 10 minutes. Add the sautéed chicken breasts to the sauce, cover and cook for about 30 minutes or until cooked through, stirring occasionally. For children remove the chicken from the bone, mix with the sauce and serve on a bed of rice.

Chicken Kebabs with Savoury Rice

Marinated and barbecued chicken on a skewer makes ideal food for a summer's day. If you are not preparing a barbecue, these chicken kebabs can also be cooked under a conventional grill. If you like you can add a variety of vegetables to the kebabs along with the chicken like button mushrooms or cherry tomatoes. This recipe will also work well with marinated cubes of lamb or beef.

Combine all the ingredients for the marinade and pour over the chicken, making sure that it is well coated. Marinate for at least 1 hour. Meanwhile, soak 8 bamboo skewers in water for at least fifteen minutes (this will prevent them from scorching).

TO PREPARE THE RICE, rinse under a cold tap and then cook according to the directions on the packet. Meanwhile, sauté the onion and peppers in the butter until softened and mix these into the rice once it is cooked.

Thread the chicken alternately with the red onion chunks on to the skewers and barbecue the kebabs about 13 cm (5 inches) from the heat for about 8 minutes, basting occasionally and turning once halfway through the cooking. Serve on the bed of savoury rice.

Not suitable for freezing
SERVES 4
4 chicken breasts or 8 boned
    chicken thighs or a mixture
1 large red onion, cut into chunks

MARINADE
22.5 ml (1½ tbsp) honey
15 ml (1 tbsp) vegetable oil
45 ml (3 tbsp) soy sauce
15 ml (1 tbsp) red wine vinegar
1 small garlic clove, crushed
    (optional)

SAVOURY RICE
225 g (8 oz) long-grain rice
1 small onion, finely chopped
½ small red and green pepper,
    cored, deseeded and finely
    chopped
25 g (1 oz) butter

Chicken Satay Sticks with Peanut Sauce

Not suitable for freezing
MAKES ABOUT 12 SKEWERS
3 chicken breasts, each cut into four
    long strips about 1.5 cm (½ inch)
    wide
MARINADE
30 ml (2 tbsp) light soy sauce
15 ml (1 tbsp) runny honey
5 ml (1 tsp) mild curry powder
15 ml (1 tbsp) crunchy peanut butter
1 small garlic clove, minced
    (optional)

PEANUT SAUCE
45 ml (3 tbsp) crunchy peanut butter
125 ml (4 fl oz) coconut milk
7.5 ml (½ tbsp) light soy sauce
15 ml (1 tbsp) brown sugar
5 ml (1 tsp) lemon juice
a little ground cayenne pepper
    (optional)

Children love eating these tasty chicken sticks which are delicious served plain or can be dipped into a scrumptious peanut sauce. Dip the wooden skewers in water for at least 15 minutes to prevent them from scorching too much under the grill.

———————

Thread the chicken strips on to bamboo skewers weaving the chicken in and out to create a snake-like effect. Thoroughly mix together all the ingredients for the marinade and marinate the chicken for at least 2 hours or overnight.

TO MAKE THE PEANUT SAUCE, combine the peanut butter, coconut milk, soy sauce, sugar, lemon juice and cayenne pepper (if using) in a saucepan and cook stirring for about 5 minutes. This sauce will keep for a few days in the fridge.

In the summer these chicken skewers are wonderful cooked on a barbecue, otherwise cook under a preheated grill. Cook the skewers for 6 to 8 minutes, turning and basting several times and serve with the peanut sauce at room temperature in individual small bowls for dipping.

Nuts about Chicken

These strips of chicken in a tasty coating of breadcrumbs and ground almonds are always popular. They're good served with spaghetti in tomato sauce.

Mix together the ground almonds, breadcrumbs and parsley and spread out on a large plate. Roll the chicken strips in seasoned flour, then dip in the beaten egg and roll in the breadcrumb mixture until well coated. Sauté the chicken strips until golden and cooked through.

Suitable for freezing
MAKES 12 CHICKEN FINGERS
50 g (2 oz) ground almonds
50 g (2 oz) fresh white breadcrumbs
10 ml (2 tsp) finely chopped fresh
   parsley
2 large chicken breasts, cut into
   6 strips
25 g (1 oz) flour
salt and pepper
1 large egg, lightly beaten
vegetable oil for frying

Mummy's Souperior Fast-Food Burgers

Suitable for freezing
MAKES 8 BURGERS
450 g (1 lb) minced beef
½ packet onion soup (25 g/1 oz)
60 ml (4 tbsp) water
freshly ground black pepper
1 onion, thinly sliced
15 g (½ oz) butter or margarine

So simple but so good to eat. My special ingredient is a packet of onion soup which gives these burgers lots of flavour. They're great on the barbecue too! Pop inside a bun with salad and relish or melt cheese on top for a delicious cheeseburger.

Combine the minced beef, onion soup, water and black pepper and form into 8 patties. Place on an oiled baking sheet and grill both sides until done (about 8 to 10 minutes). Meanwhile, sauté the onion in the butter until golden. Serve the burgers with the sautéed onions on top accompanied by Oven-Baked Chips (see page 48) and tomato ketchup.

High-Protein Chicken Burgers

Tofu lends a soft and moist texture to these tasty chicken burgers and the grated carrots add a hint of sweetness that children like. These are good served with tomato sauce.

Put the chicken, grated carrot, spring onions, parsley and crumbled stock cube in a food processor and process until well mixed. Add the tofu, beaten egg and flour and process for a few seconds until blended. Season with some freshly ground black pepper. Divide the mixture into 7 burgers, coat in breadcrumbs and sauté for 4 to 5 minutes each side or until cooked through and golden.

Suitable for freezing
MAKES 7 BURGERS
1 chicken breast
75 g (3 oz) finely grated carrot
2 large spring onions, finely chopped
15 ml (1 tbsp) chopped fresh parsley
1 chicken stock cube, crumbled
175 g (6 oz) firm tofu, drained
½ lightly beaten egg
15 ml (1 tbsp) plain flour
freshly ground black pepper
50 g (2 oz) fresh breadcrumbs

Chicken Burgers with Sage and Onion

Suitable for freezing
MAKES 6 BURGERS
a knob of butter
50 g (2 oz) sage and onion stuffing
2 chicken breasts
1 apple (eg: Granny Smith), peeled,
    cored and grated
½ lightly beaten egg
flour for coating

I like the combination of apple and chicken in this recipe – the apple keeps the burgers moist and brings out a flavour that children like. My children sometimes like to eat these in a bun with shredded lettuce, sliced tomato, cucumber and mayonnaise or salad cream, but they're also good served with mashed potato and baked beans.

_____

Pour 150 ml (¼ pint) of boiling water into a measuring jug, add a knob of butter and stir until melted. Put the stuffing mixture into a bowl, pour over the water and stir well. Set aside for 5 minutes. Meanwhile, chop the chicken breasts finely in a food processor and add the grated apple. When ready, add the stuffing mixture to the chicken and mix in the lightly beaten egg. Form into 6 burgers, roll in flour and sauté until golden and cooked through, turning halfway through (about 5 minutes each side).

Chicken Croquettes

These croquettes are crispy on the outside and lovely and soft and creamy inside. If you like you could flavour them with fresh herbs like tarragon or serve them with a tomato sauce.

Sauté the onion, celery and garlic (if using) in the vegetable oil for 4 to 5 minutes. Meanwhile, melt the butter and stir in the flour, cook for 1 minute. Remove from the heat, gradually add the stock, stirring vigorously to make sure that no lumps form. Return to the heat, stirring constantly until the mixture boils and thickens. Add the lemon juice, egg yolk and parsley and season to taste. Stir in the chicken and the cooked vegetables. Divide the mixture into 6 croquettes shaped like a cylinder and roll in flour. Lightly beat the egg white. Dip the croquettes into the egg white and then coat in breadcrumbs. Shallow fry in hot oil until golden.

Suitable for freezing
MAKES 6 CROQUETTES
1 onion, finely chopped
1 stick of celery, diced
1 clove of garlic (optional)
22.5 ml (1½ tbsp) vegetable oil
25 g (1 oz) butter
25 g (1 oz) flour
120 ml (4 fl oz) chicken stock
   (see page 20)
7.5 ml (1½ tsp) lemon juice
1 egg, separated
30 ml (2 tbsp) chopped parsley
a little salt and black pepper
200 g (7 oz) cooked chicken (1½
   breasts of chicken), finely chopped
50 g (2 oz) toasted breadcrumbs
oil, for frying

Mummy's Delicious Chicken Sausages

Suitable for freezing
MAKES APPROX. 20 SAUSAGES
1 onion, finely chopped
vegetable oil
4 chicken breasts
15 ml (1 tbsp) chopped fresh parsley
1 chicken stock cube dissolved in
   30 ml (2 tbsp) boiling water
1 apple, peeled and grated
1 egg, lightly beaten
flour
salt and pepper
75 g (3 oz) fresh brown
   breadcrumbs

MUSHROOM SAUCE
225 g (8 oz) button mushrooms,
   sliced
25 g (1 oz) butter
30 ml (2 tbsp) flour
375 ml (12fl oz) chicken stock (see
   page 20)
5 ml (1 tsp) soy sauce

If your child isn't keen on eating chicken, try chopping it in a food processor, mix it with some tasty ingredients and form it into a sausage! These are a variation on the chicken croquettes my mother used to make for us when we were children and they've now become a great favourite of my husband and children too! It's handy to keep a stock of these in the freezer. They freeze well and are delicious with baked beans or baked potato. Serve them with or without the mushroom sauce.

———————

TO MAKE THE SAUCE, sauté the mushrooms in the butter, stir in 30 ml (2 tbsp) of flour and cook for 1 minute over a gentle heat. Gradually stir in the chicken stock and soy sauce and cook for 3 to 4 minutes until thickened.

Sauté the onion in 15 ml (1 tbsp) of the vegetable oil until softened. Combine the chicken, sautéed onion, parsley, stock cube and grated apple and chop in a food processor. Form into sausage shapes approx. 7.5 cm (3 inches) long. Roll in seasoned flour, dip in beaten egg and then roll in the breadcrumbs. Heat some vegetable oil in a frying pan and and sauté the sausages for about 8 minutes or until browned on all sides.

Terrific Turkey Schnitzels

These turkey schnitzels are a great favourite and I like to serve them with spaghettini (the very thin spaghetti) and tomato sauce, preferably homemade. If you can't find turkey fillets then you could substitute chicken breasts pounded quite thin.

Place the turkey (or chicken) breasts between sheets of plastic wrap and flatten with a mallet until quite thin. Season the flour with salt and pepper. Lightly beat the egg with the milk. Mix together the breadcrumbs, grated Parmesan, parsley and herbs. Toss each turkey fillet in the seasoned flour, shake off the excess, dip into the egg mixture and roll in the breadcrumb mixture. Sauté in a mixture of vegetable oil and butter for about 5 minutes until lightly golden. These taste good with a little fresh lemon juice squeezed over them, so serve with a wedge of lemon if you like.

Not suitable for freezing
SERVES 2
2 turkey fillets (about 175 g (6 oz) each)
flour
salt and pepper
1 egg
30 ml (2 tbsp) milk
50 g (2 oz) breadcrumbs
15 ml (1 tbsp) finely grated
    Parmesan cheese (optional)
15 ml (1 tbsp) finely chopped fresh
    parsley
a few fresh or dried herbs such as
    thyme or chives (optional)
15 ml (1 tbsp) vegetable oil
25 g (1 oz) butter
1 lemon (optional)

Christine's Stir-Fried Turkey

Suitable for freezing
SERVES 4
15 ml (1 tbsp) vegetable or
    groundnut oil
454 g Bernard Mathews lean
    turkey pieces (from supermarket
    freezer cabinets)
1 clove of garlic, chopped
5 ml (1 tsp) chopped fresh ginger
10 ml (2 tsp) Madras curry paste
½ Spanish onion, sliced
½ sweet red pepper
rind and juice of ½ orange
15 ml (1 tbsp) soy sauce
15 ml (1 tbsp) sake (rice wine) or
    sherry
10 ml (2 tsp) cornflour
salt and pepper
15 ml (1 tbsp) chopped fresh
    coriander (optional)
basmati rice

My three children are all budding violinists. Having been a professional musician myself, I was keen to start them young and so they all began at the age of three learning the Suzuki method of violin. Christine Magasiner is a Suzuki piano teacher and she is also an excellent cook. This is a dish she made up after a long day of teaching which is tasty, easy to prepare and economical. It takes about 20 minutes to make.

Have all the ingredients assembled and ready, and heat a wok or heavy-based frying pan. Add the oil and heat to smoking. Put in the turkey pieces (defrost them first) and stir fry for 12 minutes; add garlic, ginger and curry paste, continue to stir fry for a couple of minutes until all the turkey has turned a pale colour; add the onion and pepper and stir fry for 2 minutes more. Mix together the orange rind and juice, soy sauce and sake and mix the cornflour into 30 ml (2 tbsp) of this sauce until smooth. Add these liquids to the pan and continue to cook, stirring occasionally for about 4 to 5 minutes or until all the ingredients are cooked through. Add salt and pepper to taste. Scatter the chopped coriander (if using) on the top and serve with basmati rice.

Oriental Beef Stir Fry

This dish can be made with a variety of vegetables like carrots, mangetout, mushrooms or baby sweetcorn. This is good served with the noodles and beansprouts on page119.

Heat half the oil in a wok or frying pan and sauté the leek and sweet pepper for 4 to 5 minutes or until softened. Remove the vegetables with a slotted spoon and set aside. Add the remaining oil to the pan with the beef and stir fry for 2 minutes. Add the soy sauce and honey and cook for 1 minute. Return the vegetables to the pan and stir fry for 2 minutes. Season with a little black pepper and sprinkle with toasted sesame seeds.

Not suitable for freezing
SERVES 2
22.5 ml (1½ tbsp) vegetable oil
1 leek, carefully washed and thinly
 sliced
1 small red pepper, cut into strips
225 g (8 oz) beef fillet, cut into strips
15 ml (1 tbsp) soy sauce
7.5 ml (½ tbsp) honey
freshly ground black pepper
5 ml (1 tsp) toasted sesame seeds
 (sauté in a dry frying pan for a few
 minutes until golden)

Spaghetti with Meatballs and Tomato Sauce

Suitable for freezing but cook the pasta fresh

SERVES 4

MEATBALLS

1 thick slice white bread

60 ml (4 tbsp) milk

350 g (12 oz) minced lean beef

22.5 ml (1½ tbsp) chopped parsley

1 small onion, grated or finely chopped

1 small Granny Smith apple, peeled and grated

salt and pepper

1 egg, lightly beaten

vegetable oil for frying

TOMATO SAUCE

1 small onion, finely chopped

15 ml (1 tbsp) chopped fresh parsley

30 ml (2 tbsp) olive oil

1 X 500 g (16 oz) carton passata (sieved tomatoes)

2.5 ml (½ tsp) sugar

1 crumbled chicken stock cube

50 ml (2 fl oz) water or wine

2.5 ml (½ tsp) dried oregano

About 350 g (12 oz) spaghettini or spaghetti

This is a really popular dish with children. I like to use spaghettini which is the really thin spaghetti. To save time you can use a ready-made tomato sauce. There are some quite good ones available made from tomatoes, onion, garlic and basil which have no additives.

Remove the crusts from the bread and tear into small pieces. Soak in the milk for 10 minutes. In a mixing bowl, combine the beef, parsley, onion, apple, bread and seasoning. Mix well and add just enough egg to bind. With your hands, shape into small balls and fry the meatballs briskly until browned all over. Meanwhile, prepare the tomato sauce. Sauté the onion and parsley in the olive oil until softened, then stir in the remaining ingredients. Bring to the boil and simmer for a few minutes. Spoon the meatballs into the tomato sauce and simmer for about 25 minutes. Bring a large pan of salted water to the boil and add the spaghetti. Boil until al dente, then drain. Divide among the plates and top with the meatballs in tomato sauce.

Annabel's Aubergine Meatballs

Adding chopped aubergine to these meatballs makes them really tasty and moist. They're good either hot or cold and are a great favourite with my children and their friends.

Salt the aubergine as described on page 35. Sauté the onion and parsley in oil until the onion has softened. Fry the aubergine slices until golden brown and chop until the flesh becomes more like a purée. Mix together the rest of the ingredients except the flour and season. With your hands, form the mixture into walnut-sized balls and roll in flour. Sauté the meatballs until browned and cooked through.

Suitable for freezing
MAKES 35 MEATBALLS

2 aubergines (about 450 g/1 lb), sliced but not peeled
1 large onion, finely chopped
15 ml (1 tbsp) fresh parsley, finely chopped
vegetable oil
450 g (1 lb) lean minced beef
½ lightly beaten egg
45 ml (3 tbsp) fine breadcrumbs or matzah meal
pinch of black pepper
pinch of salt
plain flour or matzah meal for coating

My Favourite Shepherd's Pie

Suitable for freezing

SERVES 8

2 medium onions, chopped

1 red pepper, peeled, deseeded
　　and finely chopped

30 ml (2 tbsp) vegetable oil

675 g (1½ lb) minced lamb or beef

5 ml (1 tsp) mixed herbs

30 ml (2 tbsp) tomato purée

15 ml (1 tbsp) Worcestershire sauce

15 ml (1 tbsp) soy sauce

15 ml (1 tbsp) HP sauce

300 ml (½ pint) chicken stock
　　(see page 20)

450 g (1lb) potatoes, roughly
　　chopped

450 g (1 lb) swede, peeled and
　　roughly chopped

black pepper

30 ml (2 tbsp) milk

25 g (1 oz) butter

I like to make this in small round ovenproof dishes just big enough for individual portions of shepherd's pie. A variation I like to make is adding some chopped, sautéed aubergine to the minced lamb. This is good served with baked beans.

Sauté the onion and red pepper in the vegetable oil until softened. Meanwhile, fry the minced lamb in its own fat over a medium heat until browned, mix together with the sautéed onion and pepper and chop for a few seconds in a food processor (this makes the mince softer to chew and more palatable for children). Return to the pan and stir in the mixed herbs, tomato purée, Worcestershire sauce, soy sauce, HP sauce and stock and cook over a gentle heat for 15 to 20 minutes. Meanwhile, boil the potatoes and swede, drain, mash together with milk and butter and season to taste. Season the lamb with a little pepper and arrange in one large or several smaller ovenproof dishes (eg 4 x 14 cm). Top with the mashed potato and swede, mark the surface with a fork and bake in an oven preheated to 180°C/350°F/Gas 4 for 15 to 20 minutes. Before serving, dot with butter and brown under a hot grill.

Sloppy Joes

These usually go down a treat and make a change from hamburgers. Serve on toasted hamburger buns – you can add some melted cheese to the bun if you like. This also makes a fun Mexican-style meal if you use the mixture as a filling for taco shells which can be bought ready-made.

Sauté the onion and green pepper in the oil until softened, add the meat and brown, stirring occasionally. Add all the other ingredients and simmer for 50 minutes (add extra water if it's getting too dry). Toast hamburger buns under a preheated grill (about 10 to 12 cm/4 to 5 inches from the heat to prevent them from burning). Add a slice of cheese or some grated cheese to one half of the bun if you wish before toasting the buns. Spoon the mixture on to half of each bun and cover with the other half to serve.

Suitable for freezing

SERVES 6

1 onion, finely chopped

½ green pepper, deseeded and chopped

30 ml (2 tbsp) vegetable oil

500 g (18 oz) lean minced beef

1 X 300 g (11 oz) can Heinz tomato soup

120 ml (4 fl oz) ready-made tomato sauce

30 ml (2 tbsp) tomato paste

5 ml (1 tsp) HP sauce

5 ml (1 tsp) Worcestershire sauce

2.5 to 5 ml (½ to 1 tsp) mild chilli powder (optional, just for the grown ups!)

salt and freshly ground black pepper

6 hamburger buns

6 slices of cheese or some grated cheese (optional)

POSITIVELY PASTA

Summer Lasagne

A light, fresh-tasting lasagne, this is good served with salad and fresh bread. I like to use fresh lasagne which I buy in a packet at my local supermarket. Simply immerse several sheets of lasagne in lightly salted boiling water for 5 minutes and it's ready.

First make the tomato sauce. Heat the oil in a frying pan and sauté the onion and herbs over a low heat until softened. Add the remaining ingredients for the tomato sauce and simmer for 10 to 15 minutes or until the sauce has thickened. You should have about 600 ml (1 pint) of tomato sauce. Meanwhile, steam the courgettes until just tender and cook the lasagne according to the packet instructions.

Moisten the bottom of a 20-cm (8-inch) square ovenproof dish with a little of the tomato sauce. Place two sheets of lasagne on top. Arrange half the courgettes over the pasta, sprinkle with one-third of the grated cheeses and spoon over one third of the tomato sauce. Repeat each layer of lasagne, courgette, cheese and tomato sauce. Cover with two more sheets of lasagne, spread the remaining tomato sauce on top and scatter over the rest of the grated cheese. Bake in an oven preheated to 180°C/350°F/Gas 4 for 20 minutes.

Suitable for freezing
SERVES 6
TOMATO SAUCE
30 ml (2 tbsp) olive oil
1 medium onion, chopped
30 ml (2 tbsp) fresh basil, chopped
2.5 ml (½ tsp) dried oregano
1 X 400 g (14 oz) can tomatoes
4 tomatoes, skinned, deseeded
   and chopped
10 ml (2 tsp) tomato purée
2.5 ml (½ tsp) sugar
salt and pepper to taste

6 sheets lasagne
450 g (1 lb) small courgettes, sliced
50 g (2 oz) Gruyère cheese, grated
125 g (4½ oz) mozzarella cheese,
   grated

Three-Colour Pasta Gratin

Suitable for freezing

SERVES 6

1 onion, thinly sliced

1 red and 1 yellow pepper, cored,
 deseeded and cut into thin 5-cm
 (2-inch) strips

30 ml (2 tbsp) olive oil

225 g (8 oz) courgette, trimmed and
 cut into 5-cm (2-inch) strips

450 g (1 lb) ripe tomatoes, skinned
 and chopped

1 clove of garlic, crushed

350 g (12 fl oz) vegetable stock (see
 page 21)

30 ml (2 tbsp) tomato purée

30 ml (2 tbsp) fresh basil or 5 ml
 (1 tsp) dried basil

pinch of sugar

salt and pepper

400 g (14 oz) three-colour
 spiral pasta

25 g (1 oz) butter

75 g (3 oz) Gruyère cheese,
 grated

75 g (3 oz) Cheddar cheese, grated

40 g (1½ oz) brown breadcrumbs,
 browned in a little butter

A riot of colour; the red, yellow and green spiral pasta is entwined with strips of courgettes and red and yellow pepper.

Sauté the onion and peppers in olive oil in a large heavy-bottomed saucepan until softened (about 5 minutes). Add the courgette strips and cook for 3 to 4 minutes. Stir in the tomatoes, crushed garlic, vegetable stock, tomato purée, basil and sugar. Season to taste and simmer for about 30 minutes, stirring occasionally. Meanwhile cook the pasta in a large saucepan of salted water until just tender (don't cook too long as the pasta will be cooked again in the oven). Drain the pasta, toss with the butter and pour the vegetable sauce over. Spoon the pasta into one large or several smaller ovenproof dishes. Mix together the grated cheeses and browned breadcrumbs and sprinkle over the pasta. Heat through in the oven and cook under a preheated grill until the cheese has melted and the topping is golden.

Curly Pasta with Courgettes, Tomato and Mozzarella

There are so many wonderful different pasta shapes to choose from which can be used to make this delicious baked pasta recipe. It's important to take care not to overcook the pasta, however, especially since it will be cooked again in the oven once mixed with the other ingredients. This dish could also be made using a small aubergine cut into small chunks instead of the courgettes. You will need to salt the aubergine first (see page 35) and to use more oil.

Gently sauté the onion, garlic and herbs in the olive oil until softened. Add the tomatoes, tomato purée, wine, salt, sugar and bay leaf. Bring to the boil, then reduce the heat and simmer covered for 15 to 20 minutes, stirring occasionally. Remove the bay leaf and set aside once cooked. Sauté the courgettes in the oil and a knob of butter until golden. Meanwhile cook the pasta in plenty of lightly salted water according to the packet instructions. In a large bowl, mix the cooked pasta with the tomato sauce and stir in the sliced courgettes and grated mozzarella cheese. Spoon the pasta into an ovenproof dish and top with the Parmesan cheese. Bake in an oven preheated to 180°C/350°F/Gas 4 for about 15 minutes.

Suitable for freezing
SERVES 4

1 medium onion, finely chopped
1 clove garlic, crushed
30 ml (2 tbsp) chopped fresh parsley
15 ml (1 tbsp) fresh chopped basil or
   5 ml (1 tsp) dried basil
5 ml (1 tsp) dried oregano
30 ml (2 tbsp) olive oil
1 X 400 g (14 oz) can tomatoes
10 ml (2 tsp) tomato purée
30 ml (2 tbsp) dry white wine
   (optional)
2.5 ml (½ tsp) salt to taste
5 ml (1 tsp) sugar
1 bay leaf
2 medium courgettes, sliced
15 ml (1 tbsp) oil and a knob of butter
7.5 ml (½ tbsp) oil
225 g (8 oz) pasta screws
100 g (4 oz) grated mozzarella
   cheese
30 ml (2 tbsp) freshly grated
   Parmesan

Twists of Pasta with Chicken, Mushrooms and Broccoli

Suitable for freezing
SERVES 4

300 ml (½ pint) chicken stock (see
    page 20)
½ small onion
a sprig of parsley
a few black peppercorns
2 chicken breasts, cut into chunks
225 g (8 oz) fusilli pasta
150 g (5 oz) broccoli, cut into small
    florets
15 ml (1 tbsp) sunflower oil and a
    knob of butter
1 medium onion, finely chopped
150 g (5 oz) brown cap or button
    mushrooms, chopped
1 x 295 g (10½ oz) can condensed
    mushroom soup
200 ml (7 fl oz) milk
15 ml (1 tbsp) dry sherry (optional)
50 g (2 oz) breadcrumbs
40 g (1½ oz) grated Cheddar cheese
15 g (½ oz) grated Parmesan cheese
knob of butter

There's no need to divulge that your secret ingredient is a can of mushroom soup!

Put the chicken stock, half onion, parsley and black pepper in a heavy-bottomed saucepan, heat gently and poach the chicken for about 10 minutes or until cooked through. Drain the chicken and chop finely. Cook the pasta and broccoli in a large saucepan of lightly salted boiling water until just cooked (7 to 8 minutes), taking care not to overcook them.

Heat the oil and butter in a frying pan and sauté the chopped onion and mushrooms until softened. Stir in the soup, milk and sherry (if using). In a large bowl, mix together the pasta, broccoli, diced chicken and mushroom sauce and spoon into a greased ovenproof dish. Mix together the breadcrumbs and grated cheeses, scatter this topping over the dish and dot with butter. Bake in an oven preheated to 180°C/350°F/Gas 4 for 20 to 25 minutes.

A Penne for Your Thoughts

My six-year-old daughter is a great lover of pasta, so I try to find lots of different ways to combine pasta with healthy, nutritious ingredients. This delicious bolognese sauce combines well with spaghetti or any other pasta shapes or as a stuffing for cannelloni which can then be baked in the oven covered with a cheese sauce.

Sauté the onion, sweet pepper, celery and parsley in the oil and butter until softened but not coloured. Meanwhile sauté the beef in oil until browned. At this stage, you can chop the beef in a food processor for a few seconds so that it becomes a softer texture if you wish. Combine the beef with the sautéed vegetables and add the chopped tomatoes, tomato sauce, tomato purée, wine (if using) and herbs. Season lightly. Bring to the boil, then reduce the heat and simmer covered for 20 to 25 minutes. Cook the penne according to the instructions on the packet, mix with the bolognese sauce and serve with Parmesan cheese if you wish.

Suitable for freezing
SERVES 4

1 large onion, finely chopped
1 small red pepper, diced
½ stick of celery, diced
30 ml (2 tbsp) chopped fresh parsley
15 ml (1 tbsp) oil and a knob of butter
450 g (1 lb) lean minced beef
15 ml (1 tbsp) oil
1 X 400 g (14 oz) can chopped tomatoes
300 ml (½ pint) ready-made tomato sauce (ragù)
15 ml (1 tbsp) tomato purée
50 ml (2 fl oz) white wine (optional)
15 ml (1 tbsp) chopped fresh basil
2.5 ml (½ tsp) dried oregano
salt and pepper
350 g (12 oz) penne
freshly grated Parmesan cheese (optional)

Fabulous Fusilli

Not suitable for freezing
SERVES 4
175 g (6 oz) fusilli (spiral pasta)
1 small onion, finely chopped
25 g (1 oz) butter
100 g (4 oz) button mushrooms, sliced
350g (12 oz) tomatoes, peeled,
    deseeded and cut into chunks
salt and pepper
1 egg
50 ml (2 fl oz) milk
75 g (3 oz) grated Cheddar cheese
25 g (1 oz) toasted breadcrumbs
a knob of butter

This very tasty and easy-to-prepare baked pasta dish can be prepared in advance for baking later. It is good served with buttered spinach or peas. If you like, you can add 2 small courgettes sliced and sautéed together with the mushrooms until just tender.

Cook the pasta until just al dente (it's best left slightly undercooked as it will be cooked again in the oven), drain and set aside. Sauté the onion in butter until softened (about 6 minutes), add the mushrooms and sauté for 2 minutes. Add the tomatoes, cook for 2 to 3 minutes and season lightly. Mix together the cooked pasta and vegetables and arrange in an ovenproof dish. Whisk together the egg, milk and 50 g (2 oz) of the cheese with a fork and mix this into the pasta. To make the breadcrumbs, toast a slice of wholemeal bread and make into breadcrumbs in a food processor. Melt a knob of butter in a small saucepan, sauté the breadcrumbs for a couple of minutes and stir in the grated cheese. Sprinkle this topping over the pasta and bake in an oven preheated to 180°C/350°F/Gas 4 for 15 to 20 minutes.

Spaghetti Bolognese with Grated Carrot and Sweet Pepper

Iron deficiency is the commonest nutritional deficiency in developed countries and red meat is an important source of iron for young children. However, many children don't like eating meat because it can be hard to chew. What I like to do to make meat more palatable is to brown the meat then chop it in a food processor for a few seconds so that it has a much softer texture.

Heat the oil in a pan and sauté the onion, sweet pepper and garlic (if using) for 5 minutes. Add the grated carrot and continue to cook for about 5 minutes until softened. Meanwhile, dry-fry the minced beef in a frying pan until lightly browned. Mix the minced meat with the sautéed vegetables and chop for a few seconds in a food processor to make a smoother texture. Stir in the chopped canned and fresh tomatoes, tomato purée, herbs and the stock. Bring to the boil and then cover and simmer for about 35 minutes. Season the sauce with a little salt and pepper. Top up with a little extra stock if the sauce is too dry. Meanwhile, cook the spaghettini in a large pan of lightly salted boiling water according to the instructions on the packet.

Suitable for freezing

SERVES 6

30 ml (2 tbsp) olive or vegetable oil

1 large onion, finely chopped

1 small red pepper, cored, deseeded and finely chopped

1 clove of garlic, finely chopped (optional)

1 carrot, grated

450 g (1 lb) lean minced beef or lamb

1 x 400 g (14 oz) can chopped tomatoes

4 medium tomatoes, skinned, de-seeded and roughly chopped

30 ml (2 tbsp) tomato purée

15 ml (½ tsp) dried oregano

15 ml (½ tsp) dried basil

120 ml (4 fl oz) chicken stock (see page 20)

salt and pepper

450 g (1 lb) spaghettini

Vegetarian Bolognese Sauce

Suitable for freezing

SERVES 4

1 medium aubergine, partially
 skinned and sliced (about 275 g/
 10 oz)

350 g (12 oz) tagliatelle

1 onion, finely chopped

1 garlic clove, crushed

45 ml (3 tbsp) olive oil

450 g (1 lb) sliced button mushrooms

15 ml (1 tbsp) tomato purée

1 X 400 g (14 oz) can chopped
 tomatoes

15 ml (1 tbsp) fresh, chopped
 oregano or 10 ml (2 tsp) dried
 oregano

salt and pepper

freshly grated Parmesan cheese
 to serve

Aubergine and mushrooms are quite robust vegetables and make a good substitute for minced meat. If your child is a picky eater and refuses to eat his veg, you could purée the sauce in a blender to hide all trace of the offending vegetables and call this tagliatelle with tomato sauce instead!

Salt the aubergine as described on page 35. Meanwhile, cook the tagliatelle in plenty of lightly salted water according to the packet instructions. Chop the aubergine into bite-sized pieces. Sauté the onion and garlic in olive oil for about 5 minutes, add the aubergine and cook over a high heat for 4 to 5 minutes. Add the sliced mushrooms and continue to cook for 3 to 4 minutes. Stir in the tomato purée, chopped tomatoes and oregano and cover and simmer for about 5 minutes. Season to taste with a little salt and pepper. Mix the cooked tagliatelle with the sauce and serve topped with some grated Parmesan cheese.

Spaghetti with Courgettes and Tomatoes

T his tasty combination of vegetables can also be served without the pasta and cheese and it's so good that I often serve this as a vegetable accompaniment at dinner parties. When yellow courgettes are in season, I like to mix these together with the green courgettes.

In a heavy frying pan, sauté the shallots in the olive oil for 2 minutes. Add the courgettes and cook over quite a high heat until tender and slightly golden. Add the chopped tomatoes and seasoning and cook for 8 to 10 minutes or until the sauce thickens. Meanwhile cook the pasta in plenty of lightly salted boiling water. Drain and pour the courgette and tomato sauce over it. Serve with grated Parmesan.

Suitable for freezing
SERVES 4
2 shallots, sliced
45 ml (3 tbsp) olive oil
450 g (1 lb) courgettes, sliced thinly
225 g (8 oz) ripe plum tomatoes, peeled, deseeded and chopped
salt and pepper
225 g (8 oz) spaghettini (thin spaghetti)
freshly grated Parmesan

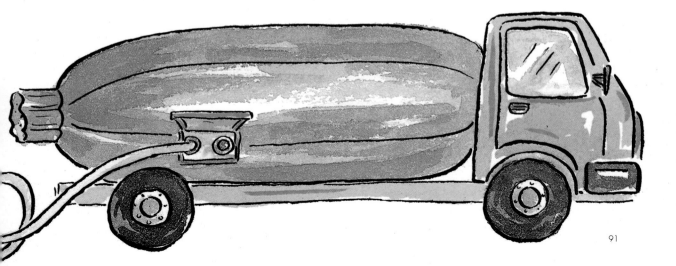

Tagliatelle with Prawns and Vegetables

Not suitable for freezing
SERVES 4
200 g (7 oz) tagliatelle
a knob of butter
450 ml (¾ pint) chicken stock (see
   page 20)
5 ml (1 tsp) lemon juice
175 g (6 oz) cauliflower, cut into
   small florets
1 medium carrot, cut into matchsticks
50 g (2 oz) mangetout or French
   beans, trimmed
25 g (1 oz) butter
1 small onion, finely sliced
1 small garlic clove, chopped
   (optional)
100 g (4 oz) small courgettes, cut
   into matchsticks
175 g (6 oz) cooked prawns, fresh
   or frozen and defrosted
15 ml (1 tbsp) chopped fresh parsley
15 ml (1 tbsp) cornflour
25 g (1 oz) grated Parmesan cheese

An easy way to turn a packet of prawns into a delicious and colourful pasta dish that everyone in the family will enjoy.

Cook the tagliatelle in plenty of lightly salted boiling water according to the instructions on the packet. When it is cooked, drain, add the knob of butter and toss the pasta in the melted butter. Pour the chicken stock and lemon juice into a saucepan, bring to the boil, add the cauliflower and carrot, mangetout or beans and cook over a medium heat for about 6 minutes or until the vegetables are just tender. Strain the vegetables, reserving the stock for later use. Melt the butter in a frying pan, add the sliced onion, garlic (if using) and sauté for 3 to 4 minutes. Add the courgettes and continue to cook for 3 to 4 minutes. Add the prawns and parsley and the rest of the vegetables and cook for 2 to 3 minutes or until heated through. Mix a little of the reserved stock with the cornflour and heat the remaining stock in a small saucepan. Mix the cornflour liquid into the remaining stock and cook stirring for about 3 minutes or until the sauce thickens. Toss the tagliatelle with the vegetables and sauce until well mixed. Serve with grated Parmesan cheese.

Pasta Twirls
with Ratatouille Sauce

When I see really nice vegetables in the supermarket, I like to make ratatouille which is a very versatile dish. I serve it not only as an accompaniment to other dishes but also as a main meal in itself combined with pasta, brown rice, couscous or bulghur wheat.

Salt the aubergines as described on page 35.

Meanwhile, sauté the onion and garlic (if using) in the olive oil for about 5 minutes, stirring occasionally. Add the yellow pepper to the pan and cook gently for 5 minutes. Add the courgette and aubergine strips and cook for 5 minutes. Add the tomatoes, tomato purée and basil. Season to taste and cook for 2 to 3 minutes. Pour in the stock and simmer covered for 20 minutes.

Cook the pasta in plenty of lightly salted water. Drain, mix with the ratatouille sauce and serve with freshly grated Parmesan.

Suitable for freezing
SERVES 4

1 small aubergine, cut into 7.5-cm
   (3-inch) strips (about 275 g/10 oz)
1 onion, thinly sliced
1 clove garlic, crushed (optional)
30 ml (2 tbsp) olive oil
1 yellow pepper, cored, deseeded
   and cut into strips
2 small courgettes, topped and tailed
   and cut into strips (about 175 g/6 oz)
450 g (1 lb) tomatoes, skinned,
   deseeded and chopped
30 ml (2 tbsp) tomato purée
1.25 ml (¼ tsp) soft brown sugar
30 ml (2 tbsp) chopped fresh basil
300 ml (½ pint) vegetable stock (see
   page 21)
salt and pepper
grated Parmesan cheese
275 g (10 oz) three-colour
   pasta twirls

Marian's Pasta and Vegetables Oriental Style

Not suitable for freezing
SERVES 4
350 g (12 oz) pasta twirls (fusilli)
45 ml (3 tbsp) vegetable oil
1 medium onion, cut into strips
2 medium tomatoes, peeled, seeded and chopped
2 medium carrots, cut into strips
175 g (6 oz) broccoli, cut into small florets
175 g (6 oz) mangetout, topped and tailed
100 g (4 oz) mushrooms, sliced
175 g (6 oz) beansprouts
4 small courgettes, topped and tailed and sliced
225 g (8 oz) fresh spinach, carefully washed
½ a chicken stock cube
30 ml (2 tbsp) soy sauce
30 ml (2 tbsp) oyster sauce
a little freshly ground black pepper

This is a great way to get your child to enjoy eating vegetables. Oyster sauce is available in most supermarkets and adds a delicious taste to this pasta dish which is very popular with my children and their friends. Feel free to alter any of the vegetables according to your particular child's likes and dislikes.

———————————

Cook the pasta for 10 to 12 minutes according to the directions and set aside. Heat the oil in a wok or large frying pan and sauté the onion until lightly browned, add the chopped tomato and cook for 1 minute, then add the carrots and broccoli, stirring occasionally for 5 minutes. Add the mangetout, mushrooms, beansprouts and courgette and cook for 4 minutes. Add the spinach and continue to cook for 2 minutes. Crumble the stock cube into a fine powder and add this together with the soy sauce, oyster sauce and a little freshly ground black pepper. Cook, stirring for 2 minutes more. Mix the vegetables with the pasta and serve.

Tagliolini with Courgettes

Tagliolini is the very fine ribbon pasta which can sometimes be bought fresh at delicatessens. However, dried tagliolini or spaghettini (thin spaghetti) is fine for this recipe if you can't find fresh pasta.

Sauté the onion in the olive oil until soft and lightly golden. Add the garlic and sauté for 1 minute. Add the parsley and courgettes and cook stirring occasionally for 8 to 10 minutes or until the courgettes are tender and lightly golden. Stir in the basil and season to taste. Cook the tagliolini in plenty of lightly salted boiling water until al dente, drain and mix with the sauce. Toss with the grated cheese and serve at once.

Not suitable for freezing
SERVES 3
50 g (2 oz) thinly sliced onion
30 ml (2 tbsp) olive oil or a generous knob of butter
2.5 ml (½ tsp) finely chopped garlic
15 ml (1 tbsp) finely chopped parsley
275 g (10 oz) small courgettes, trimmed and cut into fine strips about 5 cm (2 inches) long
30 ml (2 tbsp) shredded basil
salt and freshly ground pepper
225 g (8 oz) tagliolini
45 ml (3 tbsp) freshly grated Parmesan cheese

VEG-TO-TABLE

Ratatouille Omelette

T his concoction of sautéed Mediterranean vegetables
mixed with eggs and topped with grated cheese in the
style of a Spanish omelette is quite delicious and a meal in
itself.

———————

Salt the aubergine as described on page 35. Gently sauté
the onion in olive oil in a heavy-based frying pan until soft.
Chop the aubergine and add with the courgette and
pepper, cover the pan and cook for about 20 minutes or
until the vegetables are soft but not mushy. Add the
tomatoes and cook for a further 5 minutes. Season to taste.

Lightly whisk the eggs with the cold water, then mix in the
cooked vegetables. Heat the butter in a deep 25-cm (10-
inch) omelette or frying pan. When the butter is frothy, pour
the egg mixture into the pan and cook until set. Remove
from the heat, pour over the double cream and cover with
the grated cheese. Cook under a preheated grill for a few
minutes until golden. Leave the handle of the frying pan
sticking out of the grill and cover with silver foil if necessary.

Not suitable for freezing
SERVES 6
1 aubergine, sliced
1 small onion, sliced
45 ml (3 tbsp) olive oil
1 large courgette, sliced
1 red pepper, deseeded and cut
    into strips
2 tomatoes, skinned, deseeded and
    chopped
salt and pepper
6 eggs
30 ml (2 tbsp) cold water
25 g (1 oz) butter
75 ml (3 fl oz) double cream
100g (4 oz) Gruyère cheese, grated

Egg-stra Special Omelette

Not suitable for freezing
SERVES 1
2 eggs
7.5 ml (½ tbsp) snipped chives
salt and pepper
15 g (½ oz) butter
2 tomatoes, skinned and roughly
    chopped
25 g (1 oz) Cheddar or Gruyère
    cheese, grated

A delicious folded omelette, flavoured with chives and filled with fresh tomatoes and melted cheese. If you don't have any chives, then make a herb omelette using 1.25ml (¼ tsp) mixed dried herbs.

Beat the eggs with the chives and season with a little salt and pepper. Melt the butter in an 20-cm (8-inch) frying pan, add the beaten egg and chives and swirl the mixture around to coat the pan evenly. When the edges of the egg begin to set, lift the egg with a spatula, tilt the pan towards the edge you have lifted and let the uncooked egg flow underneath the cooked portion. Place the pan back on the burner. Spoon the tomatoes and grated cheese on to one side of the omelette. Fold over and cook for about 1 minute over a gentle heat until the omelette is set and the cheese is melted.

Easy Cheese and Onion Quiche

There are many variations to this quiche recipe. Sometimes I mix finely crushed walnuts into the pastry which gives a delicious flavour. If you like, you can vary the filling by adding some cooked chopped spinach, a little chopped bacon or ham, chopped tomato or sautéed sliced mushrooms. This is good served hot or cold with a fresh salad.

***

To make the pastry, sift together the flour and salt. Dice the butter into the flour and rub in until the mixture resembles fine breadcrumbs. Add the water and mix to a dough. Roll out the dough on a floured surface and line a 22-cm (8½-inch) buttered loose-bottomed flan tin. Prick the base lightly with a fork and bake blind (cover the pastry with greaseproof paper or foil and weigh down with dried beans) at 200°C/400°F/Gas 6 for about 15 minutes. This should set the crust without browning it. While you are baking the pastry, you can prepare the filling.

Sauté the onions in butter until softened and slightly golden. Lightly beat the eggs and stir in the cream, grated cheeses and seasonings. Remove the beans and paper from the pastry case and pour in the filling. Bake in an oven preheated to 190°C/375°F/Gas 5 for about 25 minutes.

Suitable for freezing
SERVES 6
PASTRY
200 g (7 oz) plain flour
a generous pinch of salt
90 g (3½ oz) butter
45 ml (3 tbsp) cold water

FILLING
3 medium onions, finely sliced
25 g (1 oz) butter
2 eggs
250 ml (8 fl oz) double cream
75g (3 oz) Emmenthal or Gruyere cheese, grated
25 g (1 oz) Parmesan cheese, grated
a pinch of ground nutmeg
5 ml (1 tsp) fresh thyme leaves (optional)
salt and pepper

'I Love Vegetables' Pizza Slice

Not suitable for freezing
SERVES 4
PIZZA BASE
225 g (8 oz) plain flour
5ml (1 tsp) baking powder
1.25 ml (¼ tsp) salt
50g (2 oz) butter, cut into small
    pieces
1 egg, lightly beaten
60 ml (4 tbsp) skimmed milk

TOPPING
1 large or 2 small onions, skinned
    and finely chopped
30 ml (2 tbsp) olive oil
175g (6 oz) button mushrooms,
    sliced
2 small courgettes, sliced (about
    275 g/10 oz)
salt and freshly ground black pepper
350 g (12 oz) tomatoes, thinly sliced
5 ml (1 tsp) dried oregano
15 ml (1 tbsp) fresh chopped basil
175 g (6 oz) Gruyère cheese,
    grated

A great way to get your children eating more vegetables. You can try using other vegetables too like spinach, leeks, sweetcorn or sweet pepper. You can either make your own quick pizza base using the recipe below or buy a ready prepared one.

Combine the flour, baking powder and salt in a bowl and rub in the butter. Mix to a soft dough with the egg and milk and then knead lightly until smooth. Roll out on a floured board and cover the base of a greased 33 X 23 cm (13 X 9 inch) baking tin.

Sauté the chopped onion in the olive oil for 3 to 4 minutes, then add the mushrooms and courgettes and continue to cook for about 6 minutes or until softened. Season lightly. Spread the cooked vegetables over the pizza dough and arrange the sliced tomatoes on top. Season the tomatoes and sprinkle over the oregano and basil. Cover with the grated cheese. Bake in an oven preheated to 200°C/400°F/Gas 6 for about 25 minutes.

Spotted Snake Pizza

A great looking and great tasting pizza!

___

In a large bowl, mix together the flour, salt and yeast. Make a well in the centre and mix in the egg, oil and hot water to form a dough. Sprinkle flour on to a smooth surface and knead the dough for about 5 minutes until smooth and elastic. Place in an oiled bowl, cover with a damp tea towel and leave in a warm place to rise for about 1 hour.

Meanwhile, sauté the onion and parsley in the olive oil until softened. Stir in the tomato purée and cook for 1 minute. Add the chopped tomatoes and half the juice from the can with the sugar, basil, oregano and seasonings. Cook over a gentle heat for 10 minutes or until thickened.

Once the dough has roughly doubled in size, knead for 2–3 minutes, then stretch and roll it out to form a snake approx. 7.5 cm (3 inches) wide and 80 cm (32 inches) long with tapered ends. Oil a large square baking sheet and curl the snake around it. Spread the tomato sauce and arrange the slices of mozzarella evenly along the length of the snake and sprinkle with the Parmesan cheese. Bake in an oven preheated to 190°C/375°F/Gas 5 for about 20 minutes. Place a halved olive on each cheese slice and arrange two olives for the eyes. Add the forked tongue.

Not suitable for freezing
SERVES 3
225 g (8 oz) strong white flour
5 ml (1 tsp) salt
10 ml (2 tsp) easy-blend yeast
1 egg, lightly beaten
15 ml (1 tbsp) olive oil
120 ml (4 fl oz) hot water

TOPPING
1 small onion, finely chopped
15 ml (1 tbsp) freshly chopped parsley
22.5 ml (1½ tbsp) olive oil
15 ml (1 tbsp) tomato purée
1 X 400 g (14 oz) can chopped
  tomatoes and half the juice
1.25 ml (¼ tsp) sugar
15 ml (1 tbsp) fresh chopped basil
2.5 ml (½ tsp) dried oregano
salt and pepper
125g (4½ oz) packet mozzarella
  cheese
22.5 ml (1½ tbsp) freshly grated
  Parmesan cheese
8 stoned black olives
small piece of green pepper for the
  snake's forked tongue

Puffy Pizza

Not suitable for freezing
MAKES 6 INDIVIDUAL PIZZAS
1 onion, finely chopped
22.5 ml (1½ tbsp) olive oil
1 box ready-rolled puff pastry sheet
    375 g/13 oz (36 x 23 cm/
    14 x 9 inches)
30 ml (2 tbsp) tomato purée
1 X 400 g (14 oz) can chopped
    tomatoes
2.5 ml (½ tsp) sugar
2.5 ml (½ tsp) oregano
15 ml (1 tbsp) chopped fresh basil
75 g (3 oz) sliced button mushrooms
salt and pepper
50–75 g (2–3 oz) peperoni
    (optional)
12 stoned black olives (optional)
1 egg, lightly beaten
100g (4 oz) Cheddar cheese,
    grated

Ready-rolled puff pastry makes a quick and easy pizza base. Another delicious topping that works well on puff pastry is a thin layer of passata topped with sautéed thinly sliced red onions with grated Gruyère cheese generously scattered over the top. Chicken in a Creamy Sauce with Summer Vegetables (page 61) also looks and tastes really good on this pastry base.

Sauté the onion in the oil until softened. Meanwhile, cut the pastry into six rectangles approx. 13 x 11.5 cm (5 x 4½ inches) and lay these on a large greased baking sheet. Mix the tomato purée with the onions and cook over a gentle heat for 1 minute, then stir in the chopped tomatoes, sugar and herbs. Cook for about 6 minutes or until thickened. Add the mushrooms and cook for 3 to 4 minutes, season to taste. Allow the tomato sauce to cool for a few minutes, then spread the sauce over the rectangles of pastry leaving a 5-mm (¼-inch) border all round. If using olives and or peperoni, add these now. Brush the pastry border with the beaten egg and sprinkle the grated cheese over each of the pastries. Bake for 10–15 minutes at 200°C/400°F/Gas 6 or until the cheese topping is golden and the pastry has risen.

Easy Stuffed Pancakes

Children love filled pancakes and there are many recipes in this book that can be used for tasty fillings (see page 104 for just a few). Pancakes will keep in the fridge for 3 to 4 days or can be made ahead and frozen. Making stuffed pancakes is an excellent way of turning leftovers into a delicious meal.

Mix all the ingredients together and blend for 1 minute in a food processor or blender. Pour into a jug or bowl and leave to stand for 30 minutes while you prepare the fillings. Stir again before using.

TO MAKE THE PANCAKES, lightly grease a 15-cm (6-inch) heavy-based frying pan. Place a little butter or oil in the frying pan, heat until very hot and pour off the excess fat. Pour about 30 ml (2 tbsp) of the batter into the pan, tilting the pan so that the liquid runs over the base of the pan in a thin, even layer. Pancakes should be as thin as possible. Brown lightly on one side, then turn the pancake over using a flexible palette knife and brown the second side. Transfer the pancakes on to a plate once they are cooked, stacking them with small sheets of greaseproof paper between them.

Suitable for freezing
MAKES 12 PANCKAES
100g (4 oz) plain flour or 50 g
   (2 oz) wholemeal and 50 g
   (2 oz) plain flour
generous pinch of salt
1 egg
15 ml (1 tbsp) melted butter or oil
300 ml (½ pint) milk
vegetable oil or butter for cooking

Some Ideas
for Savoury Fillings

- Small broccoli or cauliflower florets in a cheese sauce topped with toasted breadcrumbs and grated cheese or topped with a quality bought Italian tomato sauce.

- Tender Chicken Breasts with Creamy Mushroom Sauce (see page 60), chopped and topped with some grated cheese

- Chicken in a Creamy Sauce with Summer Vegetables (see page 61)

- Ratatouille (see page 35), topped with grated cheese

- Crunchy stir-fried vegetables (see page 124)

- Spinach mixed with ricotta, Parmesan and a lightly beaten egg

Simply place your chosen filling along one side of the pancake and roll up. Bake in an oven preheated to 180°C/350°F/Gas 4 for about 15 minutes. Stuffed pancakes can then be frozen in ovenproof dishes ready to reheat.

Couscous with Mediterranean Vegetables

C ouscous is quick and easy to cook and children like its mild flavour and soft texture. It blends very well with these diced, buttered vegetables.

Prepare the aubergine as in the recipe on page 35. Pour the chicken or vegetable stock over the couscous, stir with a fork, cover and set aside for about 6 minutes, by which time it will have absorbed the stock. Melt the butter and sauté the onion and sweet pepper for 4 to 5 minutes. Add the aubergine and courgette. Sauté these for 4 minutes, then add the diced tomatoes and cook for 1 minute. Fluff up the couscous with a fork and mix in the vegetables.

Not suitable for freezing
SERVES 4
100g (4 oz) aubergine, peeled and chopped
400 ml (14 fl oz) chicken stock or vegetable stock (see page 20 or 21)
175 g (6 oz) couscous
25 g (1 oz) butter
½ onion, finely chopped
½ small red pepper, diced (50–65 g/ 2–2½ oz)
75 g (3 oz) diced courgette
2 medium tomatoes, skinned, deseeded and diced

Can't Fail Twice-Baked Mini Cheese Soufflés

Not suitable for freezing
SERVES 3
40 g (1½ oz) butter
45 ml (3 tbsp) plain flour
250 ml (8 fl oz) milk
90 g (2½ oz) grated Cheddar
   cheese
1.25 ml (¼ tsp) dried mustard
   powder
3 eggs, separated
salt and freshly ground black pepper
90 ml (6 tbsp) double cream
45 ml (3 tbsp) freshly grated
   Parmesan cheese

If you always thought soufflés were difficult to prepare, then you will be surprised by how simple this recipe is. The soufflés can be prepared well in advance and then simply reheated before serving.

Melt the butter in a saucepan and use a little of the butter to grease three 10-cm (4-inch) ramekins. Stir the flour into the remaining butter and cook over a gentle heat for 1 minute. Gradually stir in the milk, beating well to make a smooth sauce. Simmer for 2 minutes. Remove the pan from the heat and stir in the Cheddar cheese and mustard powder. Beat in the egg yolks and season to taste. Whisk the egg whites in a large bowl until stiff but not dry and carefully fold them into the cheese mixture. Spoon the soufflé mixture into the greased ramekins. Place the ramekins in a roasting tin and pour in boiling water to come halfway up the sides. Bake in an oven preheated to 200°C/400°F/ Gas 6 for 15 to 20 minutes or until firm. Allow the soufflés to sink and cool. Just before you are ready to serve the soufflés, loosen them around the edges and turn out into suitable ovenproof dishes or one dish for the three soufflés (I use three 13-cm/5-inch ramekins). Spoon 30 ml (2 tbsp) double cream over each soufflé, scatter over the grated Parmesan cheese and return to the oven (preheated to 200°C/400°F/Gas 6) and bake for 10 to 15 minutes or until lightly golden.

Courgette Casserole

I love courgettes and they are a very versatile vegetable. They're good steamed, lightly sautéed in butter or cut into strips and deep fried until crispy in a light batter. This is a lovely way to prepare them and this dish can be served as an accompaniment to a meal or as a meal in itself with a crisp salad and fresh bread.

Sauté the onion in the butter until softened. Wash the courgettes, top and tail and cut into 1-cm (½-inch) cubes. Combine the courgettes, onion, cheese, eggs and seasonings and mix well. Spoon into a fairly shallow ovenproof dish (approx. 25 x 18 cm/10 x 7 inches). Sauté the breadcrumbs in the butter and mix with the grated Parmesan cheese. Sprinkle the breadcrumb mixture over the dish and bake in an oven preheated to 160°C/325°F/Gas 3 for 40 to 45 minutes.

Not suitable for freezing
SERVES 6
50 g (2 oz) chopped onion
25 g (1 oz) butter
500 g (18 oz) courgettes
50 g (2 oz) grated Cheddar cheese
2 eggs, lightly beaten
2.5 ml (½ tsp) salt
freshly ground black pepper
50 g (2 oz) toasted breadcrumbs
a knob of butter
30 ml (2 tbsp) freshly grated
    Parmesan cheese

Mini Veggie Bites

Suitable for freezing
MAKES 10 VEGGIE BITES
100 g (4 oz) grated carrot
100 g (4 oz) grated courgette
100 g (4 oz) grated potato
salt and pepper to taste
30 ml (2 tbsp) plain flour
vegetable oil to sauté

This tasty recipe will certainly encourage your children to enjoy eating their veg! These are good served with baked beans.

Squeeze out excess moisture from the grated vegetables. (The best way to do this is to lay the vegetables on several sheets of kitchen paper and then cover the vegetables with more paper and press down to soak up the excess liquid.) Mix the vegetables together in a bowl with the seasoning and flour. Heat the oil in a frying pan and fry heaped tablespoons of the mixture, flattening them with a fork to make spiky rounds. Sauté for about 5 minutes, turning halfway through. They should be golden on the outside and cooked inside.

Vegetables in Disguise

Tempura is a popular Japanese method of cooking a variety of foods in a tasty light batter. There are a wide variety of vegetables that can be cooked 'tempura style' and I find children love eating vegetables coated in this crisp and tasty batter. The other advantage is that you can't see what is inside the batter which is great for children who aren't that keen on their veg.

First prepare the vegetables of your choice. To make the batter, put the egg yolk with the ice-cold water and salt in a large mixing bowl, sift in the flour and mix well with a wooden spoon. Heat the oil in a deep fryer or half fill a saucepan to a depth of about 7.5 cm (3 inches) and heat the oil in the saucepan. Dip one piece of vegetable at a time into the batter, twirling it around to coat it, then drop it into the oil and fry until light golden. Fry only about 6 pieces at a time. Drain on kitchen paper before serving. The vegetable tempura can be reheated in the oven if you wish.

Not suitable for freezing
SERVES 4

courgettes, cut into sticks or rounds
cauliflower or broccoli, cut into small
   florets
onions, cut into rings
carrots, cut into strips about 5 mm
   (¼ inch) thick
small button mushrooms
small aubergine, sliced (see page 35)
sweet potato, cut into 5 mm
   (¼ inch) thick rounds

BATTER
1 egg yolk
250 ml (8 fl oz) iced water
150 g (5 oz) plain flour
a large pinch of sea salt

vegetable oil for frying

Pumpkin Rissoles

Suitable for freezing

MAKES 8 RISSOLES

100g (4 oz) grated pumpkin

75 g (3 oz) courgette, topped and
   tailed and grated

75 g (3 oz) grated carrot

2 small eggs

15 ml (1 tbsp) finely chopped
   parsley

salt and freshly ground black pepper
   to taste

50 g (2 oz) ground almonds

plain flour for coating

vegetable oil for frying

Pumpkins are an often neglected vegetable which is a shame as they are both delicious and nutritious. Pumpkins are plentiful in the autumn and I usually buy a whole pumpkin to carve into a face for Hallowe'en. This recipe comes in handy when I want to use up the flesh which I hollow out of the pumpkin.

Squeeze out the excess liquid from the grated vegetables (see page 108). Beat the eggs together with the parsley and salt and pepper. Combine the vegetables, beaten eggs and ground almonds. Using your hands, form into rissoles and coat in flour. Heat the oil in a frying pan and cook for 3 to 4 minutes each side, until golden and cooked through.

Deluxe Veggie Burgers

Once you've tasted these delicious veggie burgers which are packed full of nutritious ingredients you won't mind not eating meat!

Sauté the onion, carrot and mushrooms in the butter for about 8 minutes over a low heat, until softened. Add the remaining ingredients apart from the flour and oil. Form the mixture into about 10 burgers, coat in flour and sauté in the vegetable oil for 3 to 4 minutes each side or until golden.

Suitable for freezing
MAKES 10 BURGERS
1 large onion, finely chopped
1 carrot (about 75 g/3 oz), grated
175 g (6 oz) brown cap or button
    mushrooms, chopped
50 g (2 oz) butter or margarine
100g (4 oz) cashew nuts, finely
    chopped in a food processor
30 ml (2 tbsp) chopped fresh parsley
150 g (5 oz) fresh brown breadcrumbs
15 ml (1 tbsp) soy sauce
½ lightly beaten egg
a little freshly ground black pepper
flour for coating
vegetable oil for frying

Brown Rice 'Risotto'

Suitable for freezing
SERVES 4

225 g (8 oz) brown rice

1 onion, chopped

1 garlic clove, crushed

22.5 ml (1½ tbsp) olive oil

600 ml (1 pint) vegetable or chicken stock (see page 21 or 20) (dilute well if making from a cube so that it is not too salty)

100g (4 oz) broccoli, cut into small florets

100g (4 oz) cauliflower, cut into small florets

100g (4 oz) courgette, diced

100g (4 oz) carrot, diced

25 g (1 oz) butter

salt and pepper

15 ml (1 tbsp) soy sauce

Brown rice is far more nutritious than refined white rice, so it's a good idea to introduce some recipes using brown rice which are tasty and appealing. Here are two recipes for you to try. Serve with meat, chicken, fish or an omelette.

Rinse the rice and drain. Sauté the onion and garlic in the olive oil for 3 to 4 minutes, then stir in the rice and cook for 1 minute. Pour in the hot stock, bring to the boil. Reduce the heat, cover and cook for about 45 minutes or until the rice is tender. While the rice is cooking, steam the vegetables for about 6 minutes or until tender but still crisp. This is best done in a two-tier steamer with the carrots on the first level and the remaining vegetables on the tier above. Melt the butter in a frying pan and sauté the vegetables for 2 to 3 minutes. Season lightly with salt and pepper. Mix the vegetables with the cooked rice and mix in the soy sauce.

A Sweet Sensation

This delicious combination of rice with raisins and pine nuts is one of my favourite ways of presenting brown rice. It makes a wonderful accompaniment to meals or can be used as a stuffing for chicken or sweet peppers.

First rinse the rice to remove the starch, then heat the oil and sauté the onion until softened but not coloured. Stir in the rice until well coated, then pour in the stock. Bring to the boil, then simmer uncovered for 10 minutes. Cover and simmer for 25 to 30 minutes or until the rice is tender. Sauté the pine nuts in the butter until golden. A few minutes before the end of the cooking time, stir the raisins and pine nuts into the rice.

Suitable for freezing
SERVES 4
225 g (8 oz) long-grain brown rice
15 ml (1 tbsp) vegetable oil
1 onion, finely chopped
750 ml (1¼ pints) chicken or
vegetable stock (see page 20 or 21)
15 ml (1 tbsp) pine nuts
a knob of butter
25 g (1 oz) raisins

Gratin of Carrots with a Crunchy Cornflake Topping

Suitable for freezing
SERVES 4
450 g (1 lb) carrots, topped and
   tailed and sliced
1 small onion, finely chopped
50 g (2 oz) butter
37.5 ml (2½ tbsp) flour
300 ml (½ pint) semi-skimmed milk
75 g (3 oz) Gruyère cheese, grated
salt and pepper
15 ml (1 tbsp) fresh chopped parsley
65 g (2½ oz) cornflakes
25 g (1 oz) butter

Carrots are an excellent source of betacarotene which is the plant form of vitamin A. Surprisingly, unlike most vegetables, carrots are more nutritious eaten cooked than raw. This is because the cooking process helps our bodies to absorb the vitamin A that carrots contain. Both carrots and cheese tend to be very popular with children, so this combination is a real winner.

Cook the sliced carrots in lightly salted water until just tender (or steam or microwave them until tender). Meanwhile, sauté the onion in 25 g (1 oz) butter until softened. Remove from the heat, stir in the flour and gradually pour in the milk. Return to the heat and stir until thickened and smooth. Take off the heat and stir in the cheese until melted. Season to taste. Combine the cooked carrots and parsley with the cheese sauce and spoon into an ovenproof dish. Melt the remaining butter, crush the cornflakes and mix with the melted butter. Arrange the crushed cornflakes over the carrot gratin and cook in an oven preheated to 180°C/350°F/ Gas 4 for 20 minutes.

'CHOP CHOP'
FAST ORIENTAL
FOOD

Beef in Oyster Sauce with Mangetout and Baby Corn

Not suitable for freezing

SERVES 4

275 g (10 oz) lean beef steak,
  fillet, sirloin or rump, cut into strips

30 ml (2 tbsp) vegetable oil

1 small onion, finely sliced

1 clove garlic, finely sliced (optional)

30 ml (2 tbsp) finely sliced spring
  onion

100g (4 oz) mangetout, topped and
  tailed or French beans

100 g (4 oz) baby corn, cut in half

100 g (4 oz) button mushrooms,
  sliced

60 ml (4 tbsp) chicken stock (see
  page 20)

22.5–30 ml (1½–2 tbsp) oyster
  sauce

freshly ground black pepper

MARINADE

15 ml (1 tbsp) soy sauce

15 ml (1 tbsp) sake (rice wine) or
    15 ml (1 tbsp) dry sherry mixed
    with 5 ml (1 tsp) sugar

5 ml (1 tsp) sesame oil

5 ml (1 tsp) cornflour

Oyster sauce can be found in most supermarkets and adds a wonderful flavour to this beef stir fry. If you are not keen on red meat, then this could be made with strips of chicken instead of beef. Serve with rice or noodles

Mix together the ingredients for the marinade and marinate the beef for about 30 minutes. Heat the oil in a wok or large frying pan and stir fry the beef until lightly browned. Remove the beef strips with a slotted spoon and set aside. Add the onion and garlic to the pan and stir fry for 2 minutes. Add the spring onion, mangetout, baby corn and mushrooms and stir fry for 2 minutes more. Add the stock and continue to cook for 2 to 3 minutes or until the vegetables are just tender. Add the oyster sauce, bring to a simmer, return the beef strips to the wok, toss thoroughly with the sauce and heat through. Season to taste.

Beef Strips with Carrot and Baby Sweetcorn in a Secret Sauce

The secret of this delicious sauce, which is very popular with my children, is the blend of freshly squeezed orange juice and light soy sauce. This recipe takes only a few minutes to prepare but you do need to choose good quality tender meat for the best results. Serve with rice.

Marinate the beef in the mixture of orange juice and soy sauce for at least 30 minutes. Drain and reserve the marinade and mix with the cornflour and spring onions. Heat the oil in a wok or frying pan and sauté the beef for about 1 minute or until lightly browned, add the carrot and baby sweetcorn and stir fry for 2 to 3 minutes. Stir in the reserved marinade and cook stirring for a few minutes until the sauce has thickened.

Not suitable for freezing
SERVES 3
350 g (12 oz) beef, fillet or rump steak, cut into thin strips
juice of 1 orange
22.5 ml (1½ tbsp) light soy sauce
5 ml (1 tsp) cornflour
2 spring onions, thinly sliced
15 ml (1 tbsp) vegetable oil
small piece of root ginger, finely chopped (optional)
1 medium carrot, cut into thin strips
100 g (4 oz) baby sweetcorn, sliced

Chinese-Style Minced Meat with Noodles

Not suitable for freezing
SERVES 4
45 ml (3 tbsp) vegetable oil
50 g (2 oz) chopped onion
350 g (12 oz) minced meat
30 ml (2 tbsp) oyster sauce
30 ml (2 tbsp) medium-dry sherry
1 medium onion cut into strips
100 g (4 oz) carrots, cut into thin
    strips
50 g (2 oz) baby sweetcorn, cut into
    strips
100 g (4 oz) courgettes, cut into thin
    strips
100 g (4 oz) beansprouts
400 ml (14 fl oz) chicken stock (see
    page 20)
100 g (4 oz) instant Chinese egg
    noodles

I have used minced meat instead of strips of steak in this stir fry. Steak can sometimes become quite chewy whereas minced meat has a nice soft texture. The combination of oyster sauce and sherry gives this dish a delicious flavour.

Heat 15 ml (1 tbsp) oil in a wok and sauté the chopped onion for 2 minutes. Add the meat and cook until browned. Stir in the oyster sauce and sherry and cook for 3 to 4 minutes. Add the onion strips and sauté for 3 to 4 minutes. Add the carrots and baby sweetcorn and sauté for 2 minutes. Add the courgettes and beansprouts. Sauté for 1 minute, stir in 120 ml (4 fl oz) chicken stock, cook for 1 minute more and then stir in the minced meat. Cover and cook over a gentle heat for about 6 minutes. Meanwhile, cook the noodles. Bring the remaining chicken stock to the boil in a saucepan, stir in the noodles and cook for 4 minutes. Once the vegetables are tender, add the cooked noodles to the wok and cook for about 2 minutes, mixing thoroughly.

Scarlett's Chinese Noodles with Beansprouts

My four-year-old daughter Scarlett adores noodles and we sometimes call her noodle head because we think her hair is curly because she eats so many noodles! These tasty noodles are quick to make and always very popular. If you like, you can add other vegetables like thin strips of carrot or sautéed mushrooms or even some diced cooked chicken or prawns.

Heat 15 ml (1 tbsp) of oil in a wok or saucepan and sauté 25 g (1 oz) of the onion until golden. Pour in the chicken stock, bring to the boil, add the noodles, cook for about 4 minutes and set aside. Heat the rest of the oil and sauté the remaining onion until golden. Add the beansprouts and cook for 3 to 4 minutes. Stir in the noodles together with the soy sauce, oyster sauce and pepper and heat through.

Not suitable for freezing
SERVES 4
30 ml (2 tbsp) vegetable oil
1 onion, cut into strips
600 ml (1 pint) chicken stock (see page 20 or use 1 chicken stock cube)
1 X 250g packet Chinese thread noodles
1 X 350 g (12 oz) packet beansprouts
22.5 ml (1½ tbsp) soy sauce
2.5 ml (½ tsp) oyster sauce
pinch of black pepper

Chinese-Style Chicken Noodle Soup

Suitable for freezing

SERVES 4

7.5 ml (½ tbsp) vegetable oil

175 g (6 oz) chicken breast or thigh, cut into small chunks

4 spring onions, sliced

1.5 litres (2½ pints) chicken stock (see page 20)

7.5 ml (½ tbsp) soy sauce

1 large carrot, thinly sliced and cut into shapes using mini pastry cutters to stamp out shapes

2–3 button mushrooms, finely sliced

75 g (3 oz) frozen sweetcorn

75 g (3 oz) Chinese fine thread egg noodles

A popular and colourful soup. If you have mini pastry cutters, then it looks especially good if you stamp out shapes from the carrot slices before adding them to the soup. If you like ginger, then you can add a touch of fresh grated ginger to the soup. It's quite strong, so only add a little.

Heat the oil and sauté the chicken and spring onion in a saucepan until just cooked. Pour in the chicken stock and soy sauce and bring to the boil. Add the sliced carrot shapes, mushrooms, sweetcorn and noodles and simmer for about 5 minutes. Taste for seasoning and serve.

Chicken with Chinese Vegetables and Noodles

These tender strips of chicken and crispy vegetables make a really tasty, quick and easy meal. You can vary the vegetables depending on which ones your child likes best. Beansprouts, carrots and mushrooms are other possibilities.

With a fork, whisk together the egg white, cornflour and pinch of salt and mix in the chicken, turning until well coated. Heat 22.5 (1½ tbsp) of oil in a wok or frying pan and sauté the garlic for a few minutes. Add the chicken and stir fry for about 5 minutes. Remove the chicken with a slotted spoon. Add the remaining oil, sauté the onion until softened, add the vegetables and cook over a high heat for 1 minute. Add the sugar, soy sauce, sake and ginger (if using) and bring to the boil, then reduce the heat and cook for 3 to 4 minutes. Return the chicken to the wok and cook for 2 to 3 minutes. The chicken should be cooked through and the vegetables just tender. To cook the noodles, simply bring the stock to the boil in a saucepan, add the noodles, cover and remove from the heat. After 4 minutes, gently stir the noodles with a fork to separate them.

Not suitable for freezing
SERVES 4

½ egg white, lightly beaten
15 ml (1 tbsp) cornflour
pinch of salt
2 chicken breasts, cut into strips
52.5 ml (3½ tbsp) vegetable oil
1 small clove of garlic, finely sliced
½ small onion, finely chopped
50 g (2 oz) broccoli florets
1 medium carrot, cut into matchsticks
50 g (2 oz) courgettes, cut into matchsticks
50 g (2 oz) baby sweetcorn, cut in half
100 g (4 oz) shredded Chinese cabbage
1 spring onion, finely sliced
5 ml (1 tsp) soft brown sugar
15 ml (1 tbsp) soy sauce
15 ml (1 tbsp) sake or sherry
a few small pieces fresh ginger, peeled (optional)
150 g (6 oz) instant Chinese egg noodles
250 ml (8 fl oz) chicken stock (see page 20)

Easy Yakitori Chicken

Not suitable for freezing
MAKES 4 SKEWERS
45 ml (3 tbsp) sake
45 ml (3 tbsp) soy sauce
45 ml (3 tbsp) mirin
7.5 ml (½ tbsp) sugar
7.5 ml (½ tbsp) honey
8 boned chicken thighs or 2 chicken
   breasts
2 large spring onions, cut into
   2.5-cm (1-inch) lengths or 1 leek,
   cut into 2.5-cm (1-inch) lengths
15 ml (1 tbsp) vegetable oil

In Japan, yakitori bars are popular places to meet, eat and socialise. For extra flavour you can marinate the chicken in the sauce before cooking. These skewers of succulent chicken in a sweet, dark sticky sauce are a great favourite with my family. You can also add other vegetables like peppers or mushrooms to the skewers if you wish.

———————

Soak 4 bamboo skewers in water to prevent them from burning. Put the sake, soy sauce, mirin, sugar and honey into a small saucepan, bring to the boil and simmer for about 10 minutes or until the sauce has thickened. Cut the chicken breasts into chunks and thread on to the skewers alternately with the spring onion or leek. Stir the vegetable oil into the sauce and brush the chicken liberally with the sauce. Cook under a preheated grill, turning and basting frequently for 8 to 10 minutes or until the chicken is cooked through.

Colourful Egg Fried Rice

This is a great dish for using up leftover rice, it's very quick to prepare and children love it. As a short cut I use frozen mixed vegetables in this recipe, but if you have the time you can use fresh vegetables of your choice like diced carrots, red pepper and peas and steam these until tender. I often add some diced cooked chicken, meat or prawns to make it into a complete meal. For best results the cooked rice should be cold before you cook it in the wok.

In a wok or large frying pan, sauté the onion in the vegetable oil for about 4 minutes. Add the frozen vegetables and soy sauce and stir fry over a high heat for 4 to 5 minutes or until tender. Beat the eggs together with the sesame oil and season with a little salt. Stir the eggs into the pan and allow them to set, then scramble them together with the vegetables. Add the rice, toss with the vegetables, egg and spring onion (if using) and season with freshly ground pepper. If you wish add 7.5 ml (½ tbsp) more soy sauce. Continue to stir fry until the rice is hot.

Not suitable for freezing
SERVES 5
1 medium onion, finely chopped
30 ml (2 tbsp) vegetable oil
175 g (6 oz) frozen mixed vegetables, eg: sweetcorn, peas, carrots, green beans
15 ml (1 tbsp) soy sauce
2 eggs, lightly beaten
10 ml (2 tsp) sesame oil
salt and freshly ground pepper
75–100 g (3–4 oz) cooked long-grain rice (or about 150 g/5 oz uncooked if making from scratch)
15–30 ml (1–2 tbsp) finely sliced spring onion (optional)

Fresh Stir-Fried Vegetable Selection

Not suitable for freezing
SERVES 4

1 onion, finely sliced

30 ml (2 tbsp) vegetable oil

1 clove garlic

75 g (3 oz) broccoli, cut into small
   florets

2 carrots, cut into matchsticks
   (about 75 g/3 oz)

100 g (4 oz) Chinese cabbage,
   shredded

22.5 ml (1½ tbsp) water

50 g (2 oz) button mushrooms, sliced

75 g (3 oz) baby corn, cut in half

75 g (3 oz) beansprouts

7.5 ml (½ tbsp) cornflour

15 ml (1 tbsp) wine vinegar

120 ml (4 fl oz) chicken stock (see
   page 20)

7.5 ml (1½ tsp) soy sauce

7.5 ml (½ tbsp) sugar

salt and pepper

S tir-fried vegetables in this light sauce are quite delicious
  but take care to make sure the vegetables remain crisp
and are not overcooked. You can vary the selection of
vegetables you choose depending on your child's particular
favourites.

Sauté the onion in the oil in a wok or frying pan for 2
minutes. Add the garlic, broccoli, carrots and cabbage and
sprinkle with the water. Stir fry until the vegetables are
tender but still crisp. Add the mushrooms, baby corn and
beansprouts and stir fry for 1 minute. Mix the cornflour with
the vinegar to form a paste, and gradually stir in the
chicken stock, soy sauce and sugar. Add this sauce to the
vegetables and cook stirring until the sauce clears and all
the vegetables are tender. Season with salt and
pepper to taste.

Broccoli, Baby Corn and Mushroom in Oyster Sauce

A lovely combination of crisp vegetables in a delicious sauce.

Blanch the broccoli and baby corn by placing them in a large pan of lightly salted water for about 3 minutes. Drain and then rinse with cold water. Heat the oil in a wok or frying pan, add the mushrooms, broccoli and baby corn and stir fry for 3 minutes. Add the sake, soy sauce, oyster sauce, pepper and sugar and continue to stir fry for 2 to 3 minutes or until the vegetables are tender but still crisp.

Not suitable for freezing
SERVES 3
225 g (8 oz) broccoli, cut into small
   florets with the stems thinly sliced
100 g (4 oz) baby corn, cut in half
   lengthways
15 ml (1 tbsp) vegetable oil
75 g (3 oz) shiitake or button
   mushrooms, sliced
7.5 ml (½ tbsp) sake (or sherry)
7.5 ml (½ tbsp) soy sauce
15 ml (1 tbsp) oyster sauce
salt and freshly ground black pepper
1.25 ml (¼ tsp) caster sugar

Stir Fry for Small Fry

Not suitable for freezing
SERVES 3
15 ml (1 tbsp) sake (rice wine) or
    sherry
22.5 ml (1½ tbsp) light soy sauce
1.25 ml (¼ tsp) caster sugar
10 ml (2 tsp) cornflour
pepper
2 chicken breasts, cut into bite-sized
    pieces
45 ml (3 tbsp) vegetable oil
1 small onion, finely sliced
75 g (3 oz) mangetout, topped and
    tailed
75 g (3 oz) baby sweetcorn, sliced
    in half
1 medium carrot, cut into matchsticks
150 ml (5 fl oz) chicken stock,
    (see page 20)
100 g (4 oz) beansprouts
15 ml (1 tbsp) oyster sauce

A stir fry is quick and easy to make and children like the colourful crunchy vegetables. You can vary the vegetables used depending on your child's preference. To save time you could use a packet of ready-prepared stir-fry vegetables.

Combine the sake, soy sauce, sugar, cornflour and a little pepper and marinate the chicken in this mixture for at least 30 minutes. Heat half of the oil in a wok or frying pan, add half the onion and sauté until softened. Add the chicken and marinade and stir fry until cooked (about 5 minutes). Remove the chicken and set aside. Heat the rest of the oil in the wok or frying pan, add the remaining onion and sauté until softened. Add the mangetout, baby sweetcorn and carrot and stir fry for 2 to 3 minutes. Add the chicken stock and beansprouts and cook until the vegetables are tender but still crisp. Return the chicken to the wok with the oyster sauce and heat through.

Vegetarian Spring Rolls

S pring rolls are actually very easy to make and children love them. They can be made in advance but for best results, they should be deep fried at the last minute.

Spring rolls can be frozen and reheated in a hot oven. If frozen, bake for about 35 minutes and if defrosted, bake for 15 to 20 minutes. My children like to dip these into plum sauce which can be bought ready made in jars.

———————————

Heat the oil in a wok or frying pan and stir fry the onion until lightly golden. Add the carrot and red pepper and cook for 10 minutes, then add the cabbage, beansprouts, mushrooms and spring onion. Sauté for 3 to 4 minutes. Dissolve the vegetable stock cube in 120 ml (4 fl oz) water and add this to the vegetables. Continue to cook for 4 to 5 minutes. Season to taste.

Fold over one corner of each spring roll wrapper. Place 30 ml (2 tbsp) of the vegetable filling about one-third of the way down. Roll over once, fold in both ends and roll over to form a spring roll. Brush the remaining corner with some beaten egg and press down to seal. To cook the spring rolls, heat the oil in a wok or deep fryer until hot, then reduce the heat. Deep fry the spring rolls in batches for 2 to 3 minutes or until golden and crispy, then remove and drain. Serve the spring rolls hot with a dipping sauce like plum sauce, sweet and sour sauce or just soy sauce.

Suitable for freezing
MAKES 24 SPRING ROLLS
30 ml (2 tbsp) sesame or vegetable oil
1 medium onion, sliced
3 carrots, cut into matchsticks
75 g (3 oz) red pepper, cut into matchsticks
350 g (12 oz) Chinese cabbage, shredded
225 g (8 oz) beansprouts
225 g (8 oz) shiitake or button mushrooms, sliced
3 spring onions, finely sliced
1 vegetable stock cube
24 sheets spring roll pastry (from Chinese grocers)
1 egg, lightly beaten

Crispy Seaweed

Not suitable for freezing
SERVES 4
100 g (4 oz) finely shredded dark
    green cabbage or spring greens
vegetable oil for frying
5 ml (1 tsp) granulated sugar
2.5 ml (½ tsp) sea salt

Whenever I've taken my children out for a Chinese meal, their favourite dish has always been the crispy seaweed they serve as a starter. The truth is that this is not seaweed at all but in fact finely shredded dark green cabbage or spring greens and it's very quick and easy to prepare at home.

Wash the cabbage and spin it dry in a salad spinner. If using spring greens, cut out and discard any tough stalks. Place several leaves on top of each other, roll up tight and slice into long thin strips. Heat the oil in a deep frying pan (or in a saucepan) until hot, add the cabbage, stir gently and fry for 1 to 2 minutes or until a slightly darker green but do not let it burn. Mix the sugar and salt together, drain the cabbage on kitchen paper, sprinkle with the seasoning and serve immediately.

Very Easy Lychee Sorbet

A very refreshing sorbet. Serving this with a variety of fresh fruits would be a perfect way to end a home-cooked Chinese-style meal.

SERVES 5
1 X 567 g (20 oz) can lychees
50 ml (2 fl oz) freshly squeezed
   lemon juice
45 ml (3 tbsp) icing sugar

If you have an ice-cream-making machine, then all you need to do is combine all the ingredients and liquidise them in a blender. Pour the mixture into the machine and churn the mixture until frozen. However, even without such a machine this is very easy to prepare. Simply blend all the ingredients in a liquidiser or food processor until smooth. Pour the mixture into a freezer container and freeze until semi-frozen. Return the mixture to the liquidiser and process once again until smooth (this will break down the ice crystals which form). Pour the sorbet back into the container and freeze until hard. Allow to soften at room temperature for a few minutes before serving.

MICROWAVE MEALS IN MINUTES

Creamy Lettuce and Potato Soup

I f you've never tried lettuce soup before, then you may well be surprised at how tasty it is.

Melt the butter for 1 minute at Full power. Stir in the chopped onion and cook covered for 4 minutes. Add the potatoes and cook, covered, on Full power for 2 minutes. Pour over 300 ml (½ pint) of the stock and cook covered for 6 minutes or until the potatoes are tender. Wash and roughly chop the lettuce, re-cover and cook for 3 minutes, stirring once. Blend in a liquidiser and return to the dish together with the remaining stock, pepper, sugar, parsley, and bay leaf. Cook uncovered at Half power for 5 minutes. Stir in the evaporated milk and cook for 1 minute more. If you like, you can stir in some snipped chives before serving.

Suitable for freezing
SERVES 5
25 g (1 oz) butter
1 medium onion, finely chopped
2 medium potatoes (about
    350 g/12 oz), thinly sliced
900 ml (1½ pints) chicken or
    vegetable stock (see page 20 or 21)
1 large iceberg or Webb lettuce
freshly ground black pepper
pinch of sugar
1 sprig parsley
1 small bay leaf
1 x 170 g (6 oz) can evaporated milk
30 ml (2 tbsp) snipped chives
    (optional)

Gratin of Cod with Prawns and Sweetcorn

Suitable for freezing
SERVES 4
450 g (1 lb) cod fillets, skinned
salt and pepper
knob of butter
squeeze of lemon juice
25 g (1 oz) butter
25 g (1 oz) flour
300 ml (½ pint) semi-skimmed milk
75 g (3 oz) Gruyère or Cheddar
 cheese, grated
50 g (2 oz) frozen sweetcorn
75 g (3 oz) cooked prawns
50 g (2 oz) toasted brown
 breadcrumbs

A tasty combination of flaked white fish and prawns in a mild cheese sauce finished with a crunchy topping.

Lightly season the fish, dot with butter and squeeze over a little lemon juice. Put into a microwave dish and cook on Full power, covered, for 4 to 5 minutes or until the fish flakes easily with a fork. Melt the butter for 1 minute in a suitable microwave dish, blend in the flour and gradually stir in the milk. Cook for 4 to 5 minutes, stirring every minute until the sauce is smooth and thickened. Stir in 50 g (2 oz) of the cheese until melted and add the frozen sweetcorn and prawns. Carefully flake the cooked fish, making sure there are no bones and mix with the cheese and prawn sauce. Cook for 1 minute. Mix together the toasted breadcrumbs and remaining cheese and sprinkle this over the fish. Brown for a few minutes under a hot grill and serve.

Cream of Vegetable Soup

Using this basic recipe, you can make a variety of delicious soups with different vegetables. Simply substitute other vegetables like broccoli, carrots, leeks or celeriac for the courgettes. For a more creamy soup, use 120 ml (4 fl oz) single cream in place of the milk and cornflour.

Place the butter in a large dish, cover and microwave on Full power for 1 minute to melt. Add the onion, celery and carrot and microwave, covered, for 3 minutes on High. Add the potato and cook for 2 minutes on High. Pour in the stock and add the sliced courgette. Cover and microwave for 10 minutes. Transfer the mixture to a blender and purée. Mix the milk with the cornflour and gradually stir into the purée. Return to the microwave dish, cover and cook on High for 2 minutes, stirring halfway through. Season to taste.

Suitable for freezing
SERVES 6
50 g (2 oz) butter
1 large onion, chopped
1 stick celery, chopped
1 carrot, chopped
1 large potato, chopped
750 ml (1¼ pints) chicken stock (see page 20)
350 g (12 oz) courgettes, topped and tailed and sliced
120 ml (4 fl oz) milk
7.5 ml (1½ tsp) cornflour
salt and pepper

Cod in a Fresh Tomato Sauce

Not suitable for freezing
SERVES 4
15 ml (1 tbsp) vegetable oil
1 medium onion, finely chopped
1 clove of garlic, finely chopped
   (optional)
4 tomatoes, skinned, deseeded and
   roughly chopped
15 ml (1 tbsp) fresh or 5 ml
   (1 tsp) dried basil
salt and freshly ground black pepper
450 g (1 lb) fresh cod fillet
a knob of butter
30 ml (2 tbsp) crème fraîche
   or double cream

This has a lovely fresh taste and can be prepared in a few minutes. It is good served with rice or try new potatoes in season.

Place the oil in a suitable dish, stir in the onion and garlic, cover and cook on High for 3 to 4 minutes until softened. Add the tomatoes, basil and seasoning and cook covered for 3 minutes on High. Place the fish in a greased dish, lightly season, dot with butter and cook covered for 4 minutes. Mix the cream into the tomato sauce and cover the fish with this sauce. Cook covered for 1 minute.

Microwave Seafood Risotto

This delicious tomato-flavoured risotto is very easy to make in the microwave. It's a great base for a seafood risotto but it could also work well with chopped cooked chicken or served plain with some freshly grated Parmesan. Increasingly now, you can find packets of pre-prepared mixed seafood like prawns, clams, squid and mussels either frozen or fresh in supermarkets. They require very little additional cooking and would also combine well with the risotto for those children who are a little more adventurous.

_____

Melt the butter (if using) for 1 minute on high. Stir in the onion, peppers and garlic and cook covered for 5 minutes. Mix in the tomato purée, oregano and mushrooms and cook covered for 5 minutes. Stir in the rice and stock, cover and cook for 7 minutes, stir thoroughly and cook for 5 minutes more. Season to taste. Add the cooked prawns (defrost if frozen) and continue to cook on high, or until heated through.

Suitable for freezing
SERVES 4
50 g (2 oz) butter
1 large onion, finely chopped
½ small green pepper, deseeded and diced
½ small red pepper, deseeded and diced
1 garlic clove, finely chopped (optional)
30 ml (2 tbsp) tomato purée
5 ml (1 tsp) oregano
50 g (2 oz) sliced button mushrooms
225 g (8 oz) long-grain rice
600 ml (1 pint) chicken stock (see page 20)
a little salt and some freshly ground black pepper
1 X 200g packet cooked, peeled prawns, frozen or fresh

Chicken Provençal

Suitable for freezing
SERVES 4
30 ml (2 tbsp) olive oil
1 medium onion, finely chopped
1 medium red pepper, deseeded
   and cut into strips
1 clove garlic, crushed
4 large or 6 small chicken breast
   portions on the bone
1 chicken stock cube
1 X 400 g (14 oz) can chopped
   tomatoes
100 g (4 oz) button mushrooms,
   sliced
30 ml (2 tbsp) tomato purée
5 ml (1 tsp) brown sugar
2.5 ml (½ tsp) dried basil, tarragon
   and oregano
freshly ground black pepper

S ucculent tender chicken in a tasty tomato and herb
sauce, this is delicious with pasta or rice.

Heat the oil for 3 minutes on High in a large dish. Stir in the
onion, red pepper and garlic, cover and cook on High for
5 minutes. Add the chicken, coat with the vegetables and
cook uncovered for 4 minutes. Dissolve the chicken stock
cube in 50 ml (2 fl oz) boiling water and combine with the
chopped tomatoes, mushrooms, tomato purée, sugar, herbs
and freshly ground pepper in a large bowl. Mix thoroughly
and pour this sauce over the chicken breasts. Cover and
cook on High for 15 minutes. Leave to stand for 5 minutes
and serve with cooked rice or pasta.

Microwave Meatballs in Barbecue Sauce

These are really tasty and so easy to make that I'm willing to bet that once you have made this recipe you won't go back to preparing meatballs any other way.

Combine the onion, bread and stock cube and chop for a few seconds in a food processor. Stir in the grated apple and combine this mixture with the minced meat. Stir in the cold water and season. Set aside while you prepare the barbecue sauce.

TO MAKE THE SAUCE, put the chopped onion in a bowl and mix together with the oil and sugar. Cover and cook on High for 5 minutes, stirring once. Stir in the remaining ingredients for the sauce and cook uncovered for 4 minutes on High. Form the minced meat mixture into about 16 meatballs, arrange in a large dish and pour the barbecue sauce over. Cook, covered, on High for 6 minutes, turning the meatballs over halfway through. Check to make sure they are cooked all the way through. Leave to stand for a few minutes and serve with rice or mashed potato.

Suitable for freezing

MAKES ABOUT 16 MEATBALLS

1 onion, chopped
2 slices white or brown bread (50 g/2 oz)
1 chicken stock cube crumbled to a fine powder
1 Granny Smith apple, peeled and grated
450 g (1 lb) lean minced beef
30 ml (2 tbsp) cold water
a little salt and freshly ground black pepper

BARBECUE SAUCE

1 large onion, finely chopped
15 ml (1 tbsp) vegetable oil
10 ml (2 tsp) soft brown sugar
1 X 140 g (5 oz) can tomato purée
15 ml (1 tbsp) lemon juice
300 ml (½ pint) hot water
salt and freshly ground black pepper

Cauliflower or Broccoli in Cheese Sauce

Suitable for freezing
SERVES 4
275 g (10 oz) cauliflower or
    broccoli florets
30 ml (2 tbsp) water
22.5 ml (1½ tbsp) cornflour
pinch of dried mustard
300 ml (½ pint) milk
25 g (1 oz) butter
50 g (2 oz) Cheddar cheese, grated
25 g (1 oz) Parmesan cheese, grated

L ots of different vegetables go well with cheese sauce. I sometimes make this recipe with a mixture of vegetables like courgettes, tomatoes, cauliflower and broccoli.

Lightly salt the broccoli or cauliflower florets and sprinkle with the water. Cook, covered, on High for 5 minutes or until the florets are tender. Meanwhile, prepare the cheese sauce. Put the cornflour into a bowl, add the dried mustard and blend in 50 ml (2 fl oz) of the milk until smooth. Gradually stir in the rest of the milk. Cook uncovered for 2 minutes on High, whisk well, then cook for a further 2 to 3 minutes by which time the sauce should have thickened. Whisk in the butter, 40 g (1½ oz) of the Cheddar cheese and half of the Parmesan cheese. Arrange the broccoli in an ovenproof dish, pour over the sauce and sprinkle with the remaining cheese. Brown under a hot grill for a few minutes and serve.

Lamb Chops
for my Lamb Chop

My four-year-old daughter Scarlett adores lamb chops and grilled lamb cutlets. I have often made lamb for my three children and Scarlett has devoured the lot before the other two get a look in. Soy sauce is another great favourite of hers so here I've combined the two for a very simple and quick recipe. I cut the lamb into bite-sized pieces and serve it with rice.

Trim away any excess fat from the chops and place in a greased dish. Combine the soy sauce, honey, Worcestershire sauce and garlic and brush the mixture over the lamb. Lay the rosemary on top and season with the black pepper. Cover and cook on High for about 4 minutes or until the lamb is cooked to your liking.
Allow to stand for a few minutes before serving.

Not suitable for freezing
SERVES 2
2 lamb chops (about 225 g/8 oz)
5 ml (1 tsp) soy sauce
5 ml (1 tsp) honey
a few drops of Worcestershire sauce
1 small garlic clove, crushed
2 sprigs of fresh rosemary or a little
    dried rosemary
a little freshly ground black pepper

SUPERSTAR SALADS AND SNACKS

Mini Salad Bar
with Soy Sauce Dressing

S alads and a jacket potato can easily become main meals with the addition of ingredients like grated cheese, chopped egg, or chopped chicken. Combined with some delicious freshly baked breads, which can now be bought in the supermarket, fresh fruit and ice cream, it makes an easy and popular meal for the whole family. Sometimes when I have a group of children over for lunch in the summer, I lay out a salad bar with bowls of different ingredients and a choice of dressings for everyone to help themselves. The dressing below which is flavoured with soy sauce is my favourite and is particularly popular.

To MAKE THE DRESSING, mix together the first five ingredients, then whisk in the olive oil.

SOME IDEAS FOR YOUR SALAD BAR
A variety of different lettuces
Cherry tomatoes
Cucumber
Grated carrots
Sweet peppers
Tiny florets of broccoli or cauliflower
Cooked French beans
Cooked sweetcorn
Hard-boiled egg
Toasted sunflower seeds
Avocado tossed in lemon juice
Pine nuts
Tuna fish
Grated cheese or chopped blue
    cheese
Cooked pasta
Chopped chicken or turkey

SOY SAUCE DRESSING
15 ml (1 tbsp) balsamic or wine
    vinegar
a good pinch of dried mustard
a pinch of caster sugar
15 ml (1 tbsp) soy sauce
freshly ground black pepper
60 ml (4 tbsp) light olive oil

French Bean Salad with Chopped Tomato and Egg

SERVES 4

225 g (8 oz) green beans, topped and tailed

2 medium tomatoes, peeled and chopped

1 hard-boiled egg, shelled and grated

VINAIGRETTE

15 ml (1 tbsp) white wine vinegar

1.25 ml (¼ tsp) sugar

a little salt and freshly ground black pepper

45 ml (3 tbsp) sunflower or light olive oil

1 shallot, finely chopped

A lovely combination of flavours and texures. This is especially nice if the green beans are served warm. They can always be cooked ahead and reheated in the microwave.

Steam the green beans until just tender (about 4 minutes). Mix the beans with the chopped tomatoes in a salad bowl.

TO PREPARE THE VINAIGRETTE, whisk together the vinegar, sugar and seasonings, gradually whisk in the oil and finally stir in the chopped shallot. Pour the vinaigrette over the salad just before serving and sprinkle the grated egg on top.

Crazy for Cucumber

There's something about cucumber that children really love. Perhaps it's the crunchy texture. I like to serve this salad with a cheese plate. I buy miniature cheeses and cut various cheeses into sticks or thin slices and arrange them on a plate with crackers or bread and butter.

Combine the cucumber, tomatoes and chopped chives (if using) and season with a little salt and pepper. Whisk together the oil, vinegar, sugar and seasoning and pour this dressing over the cucumber and tomato salad.

SERVES 4

½ cucumber, very thinly sliced either in a food processor or by hand

3 medium tomatoes, peeled and sliced

15 ml (1 tbsp) chopped chives or finely sliced spring onion (optional)

45 ml (3 tbsp) light olive oil

15 ml (1 tbsp) white wine vinegar

a little sugar to taste

a little salt and pepper

Cucumber Crocodile

SERVES 4–6

1 cucumber

cheese (I like to use a variety of
    cheeses like Emmenthal, Cheddar
    and Edam)

1 carrot (optional)

fresh pineapple or 1 small tin of
    pineapple chunks

grapes

2 cherry tomatoes

cocktail sticks

salad cress (optional)

This looks amazing, it's great for parties and it also
makes a fabulous prop for your own children's healthy
snacks. Cubes of ham or chicken also work well on cocktail
sticks in place of the cheese.

Cut out a triangle at one end of the cucumber to make the
crocodile's mouth. Cut two lengths of cheese and the carrot
(if using) and, with a sharp knife, cut along one side of
each length to form a serrated edge. These are the
crocodile's teeth. Chop the cheeses and pineapple into
cubes. Thread cheese cubes, pineapple and grapes on to
each cocktail stick and spear the sticks into the cucumber.
Cut a cocktail stick in half and use the two halves to attach
the cherry tomatoes to form the crocodile's eyes. Give the
crocodile some teeth and he's ready to
be served up! If you like,
you can put him on a
bed of salad cress
to look like grass.

Chopped Salad

A chopped salad makes an attractive alternative to an ordinary mixed salad. If you are making this in larger quantities, then it looks wonderful arranged as rows of contrasting coloured ingredients side by side. You can pick and choose the ingredients that you like the best, finely chopped mango or turkey are two of many other possible options to include.

Peel and dice all the ingredients. Mix them together in a bowl and dress with the vinaigrette. Serve immediately.

SERVES 4

2 tomatoes

100 g (4 oz) cucumber

1 medium-sized boiled potato
  (cooked but still firm)

1 hard-boiled egg

100 g (4 oz) shredded lettuce

1 small avocado (optional)

15 ml (1 tbsp) finely chopped spring
  onion or snipped chives

½ small sweet pepper (optional)

50 g (2 oz) Roquefort cheese
  (optional)

VINAIGRETTE

22.5 ml (1½ tbsp) white wine
  vinegar

60 ml (4 tbsp) olive oil

1.25 ml (¼ tsp) Dijon mustard

1.25 ml (¼ tsp) caster sugar

salt and pepper to taste

Salad on a Stick

SERVES AS MANY AS YOU LIKE

small squares of cheese, eg:
    Gruyère, Cheddar or Emmenthal
chunks of cucumber
cherry tomatoes
chunks of sweet red pepper
chunks of carrot
chunks of celery

You could also include some
fruits like:
seedless grapes
melon balls
pineapple chunks

S erving a variety of healthy foods on a kebab or cocktail stick with a tasty dip is a great way to encourage your child to eat a more healthy diet. There are many tasty dips that you can buy in the supermarket like hummus, cream cheese and chives or guacamole. However, I find that anything that contains tomato ketchup goes down pretty well, like cream cheese and tomato ketchup or mayonnaise and tomato ketchup. The other great favourite in my house is Heinz salad cream.

Thread combinations of cheese, salad, vegetables and fruit on to skewers or cocktail sticks or for fussy eaters, who don't like mixtures, serve in small bowls for them to spear their own choice. Keep a watchful eye on the pointed ends of sticks though!

VARIATION: CACTUS CUCUMBERS
This is a fun way to present these skewers of vegetables and fruit and a good way to get your children involved. Choose a fat, straight cucumber and cut it into two unequal lengths to make one large and one smaller cactus plant. Stand the sections of cucumber cut side down on a plate and stick the vegetable and fruit skewers into the cucumbers to form the cactus needles. Surround the cactus plants with some grated carrot to look like sand!

Quick and Easy Pasta Salads

FUNNY BUNNY PASTA SALAD

Pasta, raw carrots and raisins all tend to be popular with children, so here I've combined them for a healthy and easy-to-prepare snack or light meal.

———————————

Simply mix together all the ingredients.

SERVES AS MANY AS YOU LIKE

cooked pasta, eg: pasta shells or
   waggon wheels
grated carrots
raisins
mayonnaise

SEA-SHELL TUNA SALAD

Canned tuna is always a good standby and complements the crunchy celery and sweetcorn in this salad. Sometimes I chop the tuna, spring onion and celery in a food processor for a few seconds before mixing them with the other ingredients.

———————————

Mix together all the ingredients and serve.

SERVES AS MANY AS YOU LIKE

canned tuna
chopped spring onion
diced celery
mayonnaise
cooked frozen sweetcorn
cooked pasta shells or leftover
   cooked new potatoes in their skins

Eskimo Salad

SERVES 1

2 scoops cottage cheese, plain
   or with pineapple

Fresh fruits
kiwi fruit
apple
pineapple
mango
grapes
clementines
banana
berry fruits
pitted cherries

Ready-to-eat dried fruits
raisins
dried apricots
dried apple rings
dates
pitted prunes

I remember my mother making mouth-watering platters of fresh and dried fruits accompanied by two little mounds of cottage cheese shaped like igloos using an ice-cream scoop which would be ready for me on my return from school. Choose from the suggestions here to make up your own colourful and tempting fruit platters. Toss fruits like apples or banana in orange juice before serving to prevent them from discolouring.

———————

Another good way to present fresh fruits is to cut a selection of fruits into bite-sized pieces, skewer them with cocktail sticks and serve with a small bowl of raspberry or apricot fromage frais as a dipping sauce.

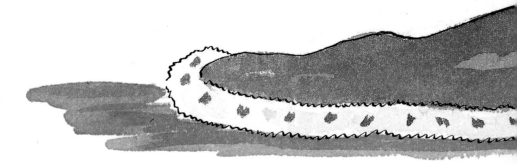

Coronation Chicken Salad

Sauté the onion in oil until softened, stir in the curry powder and cook for 30 seconds. Remove from the heat and stir in the mayonnaise, tomato purée, apricot jam and mango chutney. Put the raisins, chicken and pasta in a bowl and mix well with the sauce.

Suitable for freezing
SERVES 2
30 ml (2 tbsp) finely chopped onion
7.5 ml (½ tbsp) vegetable oil
1.25 ml (¼ tsp) curry powder
60 ml (4 tbsp) mayonnaise
5 ml (1 tsp) tomato purée
5 ml (1 tsp) apriot jam
5 ml (1 tsp) mango chutney
15 ml (1 tbsp) raisins soaked in hot water
100 g (4 oz) cooked chicken, cut into cubes
50 g (2 oz) cooked pasta shells

Noughts and Crosses

Not suitable for freezing
SERVES 2
2 large slices Cheddar cheese or
    50 g (2 oz) grated cheese, eg:
    Gruyère, Edam or Cheddar
2 slices bread, toasted
8 cooked French beans
3 cherry tomatoes
small piece of green pepper, cut into
    thin 2.5-cm (1-inch) strips

This is a fun snack to make when your child has a friend over for tea.

Lay the cheese slices on top of the toast and cook under a preheated grill for 3 to 4 minutes or until the cheese has melted and is slightly golden. Put the toasted cheese on serving plates, arrange the green beans to form a grid for the noughts and crosses and make the noughts from halved cherry tomatoes and the crosses from crossed strips of green pepper.

10-Minute French Bread Pizzas

Halved baguettes make an excellent ready-made pizza base. You could also try using granary baguettes or ciabatta bread as a pizza base. Add extra toppings like sautéed sliced mushrooms or anchovies if you wish.

Cut the baguettes in half lengthways and lightly toast the cut side of the bread under a preheated grill for 2 to 3 minutes. Spread the tomato sauce over the toasted side of the baguette and arrange the sliced tomatoes and mozzarella cheese alternately along the length of the baguette halves. Season lightly and top with the olive rings, basil and Parmesan cheese. Drizzle over a little olive oil and place under a preheated grill for about 5 minutes or until the cheese is bubbling and golden.

Not suitable for freezing
MAKES 2 FRENCH BREAD
   PIZZA HALVES
1 X 30-cm (12-inch) baguette
120 ml (4 fl oz) thick tomato sauce, homemade (see Spotted Snake Pizza topping page 101) or bought
2 tomatoes, thinly sliced
100 g (4 oz) mozzarella cheese, thinly sliced
salt and pepper
4 stoned black olives, cut into rings (optional)
4 fresh basil leaves, shredded
7.5 ml (½ tbsp) freshly grated Parmesan cheese
olive oil for drizzling

Puffy Cheese Toasties

Not suitable for freezing
SERVES 4
25 g (1 oz) butter
15 ml (1 tbsp) plain flour
150 ml (¼ pint) semi-skimmed milk
150 ml (3 oz) Edam, Gouda or
    Cheddar cheese, grated
1.25 ml (¼ tsp) dried mustard
5 ml (1 tsp) Worcestershire sauce
2 eggs, separated
4 slices wholemeal bread or
    multi-grain white bread
2 tomatoes, thinly sliced (optional)

Serve this tasty cheese topping plain or topped with thinly sliced tomatoes. For a more substantial meal, grill the cheese and then place a poached egg on top.

Melt half the butter in a small saucepan, stir in the flour and cook for 1 minute. Gradually stir in the milk, bring to the boil and then simmer until thickened. Remove from the heat, stir in the grated cheese, mustard and Worcestershire sauce and egg yolks. Whisk the egg whites until stiff then fold into the cheese mixture. Toast the bread, spread with the remaining butter and top with the cheese mixture. Arrange some sliced tomatoes on top (if using) and cook in an oven preheated to 190°C/375°F/Gas 5 for 15 minutes or until puffy and golden.

Apple Smiles

T his snack is easy to prepare and will certainly bring a smile to your child's face!

Spread peanut butter on one side of each apple slice (squeeze a little lemon juice over the apple if not serving immediately). Place four miniature marshallows or cubes of cheese on one apple slice and then lay another apple slice peanut butter side down on top. If you like, add an apricot to form the tongue.

Not suitable for freezing
MAKES 4 APPLE SMILES
1 red apple, cored and sliced into
    eighths
a squeeze of lemon juice
smooth peanut butter
miniature marshmallows or small
    cubes of cheese (for a healthier
    alternative)
dried apricots for the tongues
    (optional)

Dressing for Dinner

Suitable for freezing

SERVES 5

25 g (1 oz) finely chopped onion

50 ml (2 fl oz) vegetable oil

30 ml (2tbsp) rice wine vinegar

30 ml (2 tbsp) water

15 ml (1 tbsp) chopped fresh ginger
   root

15 ml (1 tbsp) chopped celery

15 ml (1 tbsp) soy sauce

7.5 ml (1½ tsp) tomato purée

7.5 ml (1½ tsp) sugar

5 ml (1 tsp) lemon juice

salt and pepper

The secret of getting your child to enjoy eating salad is to find an irresistible salad dressing. This one is pure magic, and I can't make enough of it to please my children. It is based on the salad dressing served at a chain of popular American Japanese restaurants called Benihana. I use it to dress a mixed salad comprising crisp mixed lettuce, tomatoes, grated carrot, cucumber and sometimes thinly sliced radish. Once you've tried this recipe you will probably want to increase the quantities and keep a bottle full in your fridge.

Combine all the ingredients in a blender or food processor and process until smooth.

QUICK
HOME-BAKED
CAKES

The Ultimate Chocolate Cake

Suitable for freezing
SERVES 8–10
175 g (6 oz) unsalted butter
190 g (6½ oz) caster sugar
5 eggs, separated
250 g (9 oz) good quality plain dark
    chocolate
45 ml (3 tbsp) dark rum
75 g (3 oz) ground almonds
75 g (3 oz) plain flour

ICING
75 g (3 oz) dark chocolate
30 ml (2 tbsp) rum
75 g (3 oz) unsalted butter

RASPBERRY COULIS
450 g (1lb) fresh or frozen
    raspberries
90–120 ml (6–8 tbsp) icing
    sugar

I tried and tested many ideas for chocolate cakes before selecting this as the best. It has a rich chocolaty taste with a mousse-like texture.

Beat together the butter and sugar until fluffy, then stir in the egg yolks. Meanwhile, melt the chocolate either in a microwave or in a double boiler and stir in the rum. Beat the melted chocolate into the egg yolk mixture. In a separate bowl, whisk the egg whites until stiff. Gently fold some of the egg whites into the chocolate mixture, alternating with some of the ground almonds and flour until all the ingredients have been used up. Grease and line a 23-cm (9-inch) cake tin with a push-up base, pour the mixture into the tin and bake for 25 to 30 minutes at 180°C/350°F/Gas 4. Remove and leave to cool.

TO PREPARE THE RASPBERRY COULIS, purée the raspberries in a blender, then sieve into a small saucepan. Add the sugar to taste and stir over a low heat until the sugar has dissolved.

TO PREPARE THE ICING, melt the remaining chocolate, stir in the rum and beat in the butter. Spread the glossy sauce over the cake, making attractive swirls with a palette knife. Serve with a little of the raspberry coulis.

Heaven-sent Chocolate Cake

This cake takes only a few minutes to prepare in a food processor and the rum-flavoured filling and chocolate flake topping is scrumptious and simple to make. It's a great favourite with my family especially my son Nicholas.

Stir the cocoa into the boiling water until dissolved. Pour into the bowl of an electric mixer and add the margarine, sugar, eggs, flour and baking powder and beat for 2 to 3 minutes. Divide the mixture in half and spoon into two greased and lined 20-cm (8-inch) sandwich tins. Smooth the top of the cakes with a spatula and bake in an oven preheated to 180°C/350°F/Gas 4 for 30 minutes. Allow to cool, then turn out on to a wire rack.

Meanwhile, prepare the filling. Melt the chocolate and rum in a suitable dish in a microwave or in a double boiler over hot water. Remove from the heat, allow to cool a little and stir in the soured cream. Whip the double cream until it forms soft peaks and fold in the chocolate mixture. The filling will be quite thick. Once the cakes are cool, spread this filling over one of the cakes and place the second cake on top. To prepare the topping, simply melt the chocolate and stir in the soured cream and icing sugar. Spread the frosting on top of the cake and, if you like, sprinkle with the Cadbury's flake broken into little pieces. Set aside in the fridge for several hours until the filling is firm.

Suitable for freezing
SERVES 8–10
25 g (1 oz) cocoa powder
60 ml (2 fl oz) boiling water
200 g (8 oz) soft margarine
200 g (8 oz) caster sugar
4 eggs
200 g (8 oz) self-raising flour
10 ml (2 tsp) baking powder

CHOCOLATE RUM MOUSSE FILLING
200 g (7 oz) good quality plain chocolate
30 ml (2 tbsp) dark rum or 5 ml (1 tsp) imitation rum flavouring
1 X 142 ml (5 fl oz) carton soured cream
300 ml (½ pint) double cream

CHOCOLATE FLAKE TOPPING
100 g (4 oz) plain chocolate
120 ml (4 fl oz) soured cream
90 ml (6 tbsp) icing sugar
1 Cadbury's Flake (optional)

Nicholas's Favourite Marble Cake

Suitable for freezing

SERVES 10

225 g (8 oz) butter, room temperature

225 g (8 oz) caster sugar

75 g (3 oz) ground almonds

175 g (6 oz) sifted self-raising flour

4 eggs

45 ml (3 tbsp) milk

5 ml (1 tsp) almond essence

5 ml (1 tsp) finely grated orange rind

75 g (3 oz) plain chocolate, broken
   into pieces

15 ml (1 tbsp) cocoa powder

Creating a marbled effect is very easy once you know how and this is a cake that never fails to please. My son Nicholas loves this cake and he likes to eat a slice when he comes home from school before he starts his homework. It's lovely and moist and flavoured with almonds, chocolate and a hint of orange.

———————

Cream the butter and sugar together until fluffy. Sieve the almonds and flour and add to the mixture. Gradually beat in the eggs one at a time and add the milk. Transfer half the cake mixture to another bowl and stir in the almond essence and orange rind. Melt the chocolate in a microwave or double boiler, and stir the melted chocolate and sifted cocoa powder into the remaining cake mixture. This looks best when baked in a 20-cm (8-inch) ring tin, fluted for the prettiest effect. Grease and flour the tin first or use a non-stick baking spray. Alternatively, line a 900 g (2 lb) oblong cake tin or a 20-cm (8-inch) round tin and pour in the batter. Spoon alternate layers of the cake mixture into the tin and use a skewer or a knife to swirl through the mixture to give a marbled effect. Level the surface and bake for about 1 hour at 170°C/325°F/Gas 3 or until the cake is well risen and golden. Turn out on to a wire rack and cool.

Caribbean Chocolate Cake

A lovely combination of dark chocolate and moist coconut that melts in the mouth. This is one of my favourites!

Break the chocolate into pieces and melt either in a microwave or in a bowl over simmering water. In a mixing bowl combine the yolks and the sugar and beat until creamy. Beat in the softened butter and the melted chocolate. Mix in the coconut, rum, cinnamon, vanilla, lemon zest and cornflour. In a clean bowl, beat the egg whites until stiff and carefully fold these into the chocolate mixture. Turn into a greased round 20-cm (8-inch) cake mould with a depth of about 4 cm (1½ inches) and bake in an oven preheated to 180°C/350°F/Gas 4 for about 35 minutes. Allow to cool for 10 minutes, then turn out on to a wire rack.

Suitable for freezing
SERVES 8

150g (5 oz) good quality dark chocolate
4 eggs, separated
100 g (4 oz) caster sugar
125 g (4½ oz) softened butter
125 g (4½ oz) desiccated coconut
30 ml (2 tbsp) dark rum
2.5 ml (½ tsp) powdered cinnamon
5 ml (1 tsp) vanilla esssnce
5 ml (1 tsp) lemon zest
15 ml (1 tbsp) cornflour

159

Lemon and Strawberry Cheesecake

Not suitable for freezing
SERVES 10
225 g (8 oz) digestive biscuits,
    crushed
150 g (5 oz) butter
½ X 135 g (4¾ oz) packet lemon jelly
200 g (7 oz) cottage cheese
175 g (6 oz) cream cheese
1 X 397 g (14 oz) can condensed milk
juice of 1 lemon
225 g (8 oz) fresh strawberries

DECORATION
50 g (2 oz) strawberries and 2
    peeled and sliced kiwi fruit.

A lovely combination of lemon cheesecake and fresh summer berries.

Crush the digestive biscuits in a food processor. Melt the butter and stir the melted butter into the biscuit crumbs. Line a 20-cm (8-inch) springform cake tin with greaseproof paper and spoon the crumbs over the base, pressing down well. Dissolve the jelly in 120 ml (4 fl oz) boiling water and set aside to cool. Put the cottage cheese in a food processor and blend for about 30 seconds. Add the cream cheese and condensed milk and blend until smooth. Stir in the cooled jelly mixture and fresh lemon juice. Roughly chop the strawberries and scatter them over the biscuit base. Pour the cream cheese mixture over the fruit and put in the fridge to set. Decorate around the edge of the cheesecake with sliced strawberries and kiwi fruit.

Quick and Easy No-Bake Raspberry Cheesecake

T his makes a very light, soft and creamy cheesecake, it's absolutely delicious and can be made in 15 minutes.

Not suitable for freezing
SERVES 6–8
175 g (6 oz) digestive biscuits
65 g (2½ oz) butter, melted
5 ml (1 tsp) gelatine
300 ml (10 fl oz) thick double cream
90 g (3½ oz) icing sugar
200 g (7 oz) cream cheese
450 g (1 lb) frozen raspberries
30 ml (2 tbsp) raspberry jam
37.5 ml (2½ tbsp) caster sugar
15 ml (1 tbsp) cornflour

Crush the biscuits in a food processor or with a rolling pin and mix with the butter. Line a 20-cm (8-inch) loose-bottomed tin and press the crushed biscuits on to the base. Sprinkle the gelatine over 30 ml (2 tbsp) of very hot water in a tea cup and stir until completely dissolved. If it has not fully dissolved, stand the cup in a pan of warm water over a low heat and stir until it has. Beat the cream with the icing sugar until stiff, gently fold in the cream cheese and gelatine until blended and spoon this mixture over the biscuit base.

TO MAKE THE TOPPING, thaw the raspberries and put 225 g (8 oz) raspberries in a small saucepan together with the raspberry jam and caster sugar. Cook over a gentle heat until the sugar has dissolved and the raspberries are mushy. Sieve the raspberry mixture and mix a little of the purée with the cornflour, stirring until smooth. Gently heat the rest of the purée in a saucepan, stir in the cornflour mixture and cook, stirring over a gentle heat, until thickened. Add the remaining whole raspberries and set aside to cool. Spread the raspberry topping over the cake and put in the fridge to set.

Julie's French Apple Cake

Suitable for freezing

SERVES 8

5 small eating apples

1 lemon

200 g (7 oz) softened butter

225 g (8 oz) caster sugar

4 eggs

200 g (7 oz) plain flour

5 ml (1 tsp) baking powder

100 g (4 oz) fine-cut desiccated
   coconut

A light sponge cake flavoured with moist coconut and succulent apples.

Peel and core the apples, cut them in half and squeeze the lemon juice over them. Beat together the butter and sugar until creamy, then beat in the eggs one by one. Mix in the flour, baking powder and 70 g (2¾ oz) of the coconut. Grease a 23-cm (9-inch) cake tin and pour the mixture into the tin. With a sharp knife, score the curved sides of the apples about 5 times without actually cutting through to the middle. Arrange the halved apples in a circle, curved side up, pressing down lightly into the cake batter until just covered. Sprinkle the remaining coconut over the surface of the cake and bake in an oven preheated to 170°C/325°F/Gas 3 for 50 minutes.

Best-Ever Carrot Cake

This has to be one of the most delicious carrot cakes I have ever tasted and I'm particularly partial to carrot cake myself! It's a super cake to make for a special occasion. If you would prefer to make a smaller cake simply halve the quantities and make one 20-cm (8-inch) cake

---

Sift together the flour, baking powder, bicarbonate of soda, salt and cinnamon. In a mixing bowl beat together the eggs, sugar, oil and vanilla essence until well blended. Stir in the grated carrots, crushed pineapple, nuts and raisins. Butter and flour two 20-cm (8-inch) sandwich tins, divide the cake mixture between the two tins and bake in an oven pre-heated to 180°C/350°F/Gas 4 for 45 minutes. Turn out the cakes and cool on a wire rack.

TO MAKE THE ICING, beat together the butter, sugar and vanilla. Stir in the cream cheese until blended but don't over beat or the icing will become too watery (if for some reason the icing is too soft, leave it in the fridge to harden before icing the cake). Level the top of one of the cakes with a sharp knife and spread a thin layer of icing over the cake. Place the second cake on top to form a sandwich. Spread the rest of the icing over the top and sides of the cake, making swirling patterns on the top of the cake with a palette knife.

Suitable for freezing without the icing
SERVES 8–10

175 g (6 oz) plain flour

10 ml (2 tsp) baking powder

5 ml (1 tsp) bicarbonate of soda

5 ml (1 tsp) salt

10 ml (2 tsp) cinnamon

4 eggs

300 g (10½ oz) caster sugar

350 ml (12 fl oz) vegetable oil

5 ml (1 tsp) vanilla essence

215 g (7½ oz) grated carrots

1 x 250 g (9 oz) can crushed
    pineapple, drained

65 g (2½ oz) chopped pecans or
    walnuts

100 g (4 oz) raisins

ICING

65 g (2½ oz) unsalted butter

250 g (9 oz) icing sugar

1.25 ml (¼ tsp) vanilla essence

125 g (4½ oz) cream cheese

One-Bowl Victoria Sandwich Cake

Suitable for freezing unfilled
SERVES 6
150 g (5 oz) soft margarine
150 g (5 oz) caster sugar
3 eggs
pinch of salt
175 g (6 oz) self-raising flour

FILLING
150 ml (5 fl oz) double cream
60–75 ml (4–5 tbsp) raspberry
   or strawberry jam
icing sugar, to finish

This Victoria sponge cake filled with raspberry or strawberry jam and fresh cream is one of those old-fashioned favourites that everyone loves. All the ingredients are mixed together in one bowl and then baked in the oven and the results are perfect every time.

Combine all the ingredients for the cake and beat in an electric mixer until thoroughly blended. Line and grease two round 18-cm (7-inch) sandwich tins. Divide the batter between them and level the surface of each cake with a spatula. Bake in an oven preheated to 180°C/350°F/ Gas 4 for 25 to 30 minutes. The cakes are cooked when they are well risen and the sponge springs back when lightly pressed. Allow the cakes to cool for a few minutes and then turn out on to a wire rack. Whip the double cream until it stands up in soft peaks. When cold, spread the jam over the surface of one of the cakes, top with the whipped cream and put the second cake on top. Lift on to a serving plate and sift some icing sugar over the top of the cake.

Light-as-a-Feather Lemon Cake

A n unusual melt-in-the-mouth lemon cake with a sherry-soaked base. For older children and adults only!

Crush the boudoir biscuits (this is best done by putting them in a plastic bag and crushing them with a rolling pin). Put the crushed biscuits into a bowl and pour over enough sherry to soak them. Grate the zest of the lemons (take care to grate the skin only and not the pith) and squeeze the lemons. Separate the eggs. Put the egg yolks, 150 g (5 oz) of the sugar, the lemon juice and lemon zest in the top of a double boiler and gently heat over simmering water until thickened. Beat the egg whites together with the remaining sugar in an electric mixer until stiff. Pour 120 ml (4 fl oz) of water on to the gelatine and stir until dissolved. Stir the gelatine into the lemon mixture and allow to cool down. Once cool, fold the egg whites into the lemon mixture.

Line a 23-cm (9-inch) springform cake tin and press the crushed boudoir biscuits on to the base of the tin. Pour the lemon mixture over the biscuits and set aside in the fridge to set. Once set, decorate the top with the drained mandarin oranges.

Not suitable for freezing
SERVES 8–10
1 X 250 g (9 oz) packet of boudoir biscuits
sherry
2 large or 3 small lemons
8 eggs
200 g (7 oz) caster sugar
1 packet of gelatine
2 X 295 g (10½ oz) cans mandarin oranges

'Can't-Go-Wrong' Golden Syrup Cake

Suitable for freezing
SERVES 8
175 ml (6 fl oz) corn oil
175 ml (6 fl oz) golden syrup
3 eggs, lightly beaten
175 ml (6 fl oz) cold water
225 g (8 oz) self-raising flour
7.5 ml (1½ tsp) ground cinnamon
7.5 ml (1½ tsp) mixed spice
2.5 ml (½ tsp) ground ginger
5 ml (1 tsp) bicarbonate of soda
175 g (6 oz) soft brown sugar
75 g (3 oz) raisins or sultanas

My friend Louise Fox gave me the recipe for this cake. She has two children and is a fitness instructor so she leads a very busy life and likes recipes that are quick and easy to prepare. This one is always popular with children. You can also make this into a honey cake if you substitute honey for the golden syrup.

Mix together the oil, golden syrup, eggs and water. Sift together the flour, cinnamon, mixed spice, ginger and bicarbonate of soda and stir in the sugar. Combine the wet ingredients with the dry ingredients and stir in the raisins or sultanas. Grease and line a 20-cm (8-inch) round cake tin. Pour the cake mix into the tin and bake in an oven preheated to 170°C/375°F/Gas 3 for 1 hour, or until a skewer inserted into the middle of the cake comes out dry.

SWEET SURRENDER

Rhubarb Crumble

Suitable for freezing
SERVES 4
675 g (1½ lb) trimmed rhubarb, cut
    into 2.5-cm (1-inch) sticks
65 g (2½ oz) caster sugar
2.5 ml (½ tsp) cinnamon (optional)

CRUMBLE TOPPING
175 g (6 oz) plain flour
1.25 ml (¼ tsp) salt
100 g (4 oz) cold butter, chopped
100 g (4 oz) demerera sugar

Old-fashioned comfort food at its best, delicious with hot custard or vanilla ice cream. Other good fruits to try are cooking apples, on their own or with blackberries (frozen or fresh), apricots, gooseberries or juicy fresh plums when they are in season. Adjust the amount of sugar you add to the fruit depending on how sweet you like it to be.

Prepare the rhubarb, mix with the sugar and cinnamon and place in a buttered, fairly shallow ovenproof dish approximately 20 cm (8 inches) square. To make the crumble topping, mix together the flour and salt and rub in the butter with your fingertips until the mixture resembles coarse crumbs, then stir in the sugar. Sprinkle the topping over the fruit and press down lightly. Bake in an oven preheated to 200°C/400°F/Gas 6 for about 35 minutes or until lightly golden.

Louise's Apple and Blackberry Pudding

Louise is a good friend of mine who has two children, Olivia and Ben, both of whom are very fussy eaters. This is one of her children's favourite desserts and it's quick and easy to make. Blackberries are rich in Vitamin C and my children love them. Here the slightly tart flavour of the fruit blends really well with the almond sponge topping. Serve hot on its own or with custard or vanilla ice cream.

Cream together the butter and sugar and beat in the eggs, ground almonds and almond essence. Mix together the fruit and place in an ovenproof dish. Spread the topping over the fruit and bake in an oven preheated to 170°C/325°F/Gas 3 for 45 minutes.

Not suitable for freezing
SERVES 4
100 g (4 oz) butter
100 g (4 oz) caster sugar
2 eggs
100 g (4 oz) ground almonds
5 ml (1 tsp) almond essence
450 g (1 lb) cooking apples, peeled and sliced
225 g (½ lb) blackberries, fresh or frozen

Flipping Good Pancakes ...

Suitable for freezing
MAKES ABOUT 15 PANCAKES
100 g (4 oz) plain flour
pinch of salt
15 ml (1 tbsp) caster or icing sugar
2 eggs (size 2)
175 ml (6 fl oz) milk
50 ml (2 fl oz) water
30 ml (2 tbsp) melted butter
vegetable oil for frying

Children seem to adore pancakes, they are quick and easy to make and can be frozen as long as they are separated with sheets of wax or special freezer paper. My children love them drizzled with maple syrup and served with ice cream but you can also try some of the tempting variations that follow.

———————

Sift the flour, salt and sugar into a bowl. Make a well in the centre and add the eggs and half the milk. Using a whisk, beat the ingredients until smooth. Whisk in the rest of the milk and the water to make a smooth batter, then stir in the melted butter.

I like to make quite small pancakes, so I use an 18- or 20-cm (7- or 8-inch) non-stick frying pan, however a larger frying pan will do if you don't have one that size. Heat a very small amount of oil in the frying pan, pour in 30–45 ml (2–3 tbsp) of the batter, swirling it around the frying pan quickly so that it covers the base. Cook the pancake for 20 to 30 seconds until it is golden brown underneath, then turn it over with a spatula or flip it into the air and catch it with the pan! Cook for 20 to 30 seconds on the other side until golden and slide it on to a plate. Cook the rest of the pancakes and add a little more oil if the batter starts sticking to the pan.

… and the Seven Wonders of the World

There are many different ways to eat pancakes, why not try some of these:

1   Sprinkle with icing sugar and lemon juice.

2   Fill with hot stewed cooking apple or apple purée and serve with vanilla ice cream.

3   Cover with sliced bananas and drizzle over maple syrup or chocolate sauce.

4   Serve with canned black cherries thickened with arrowroot and a scoop of Greek yogurt or vanilla ice cream.

5   Fill with fresh fruit and drizzle over some golden syrup or serve with yogurt and honey.

6   Make up strawberry or raspberry jelly, chop the jelly and mix with sliced strawberries or fresh raspberries. Fill the pancake with the chopped jelly and fruit and serve with vanilla ice cream.

7   Spread with a little raspberry jam, add some sliced fresh peach or drained canned peaches and fold the pancake in half. Serve with vanilla ice cream.

Jelly Baby

Not suitable for freezing
SERVES 8
2 X 135 g (4¾ oz) packets
   raspberry jelly
1 X 425 g (15 oz) can pitted black
   cherries
100 g (4 oz) fresh or frozen
   raspberries
100 g (4 oz) fresh or frozen
   blueberries

For me, jelly is the ultimate comfort food and red jelly with summer fruits set in an old-fashioned jelly mould is, I think, probably one of the most popular children's desserts ever invented. Delicious served with vanilla ice cream.

Break the jelly into squares and place in a large measuring jug. Pour in boiling water up to the 600-ml (1-pint) mark and stir until dissolved. Stir in 450 ml (¾ pint) of cold water. Drain the cherries and add to the jelly together with the fresh raspberries and blueberries. Pour into a mould or serving dish and, when cool, put in the fridge to set.

Frozen Yogurt Ice Cream

I adore frozen yogurt ice cream and this tastes so good that you don't really need any extra flavourings. However, if you like you could add fruit purées to flavour the frozen yogurt like the summer berry flavour below. For best results, I make this in an ice-cream maker but you can also make it without. Simply put the mixture in a carton in the freezer, and stir or beat in a mixer or food processor two or three times during the freezing process to break up the ice crystals. It's fun to make Knickerbocker Glories combining scoops of frozen yogurt with fresh berries.

SERVES 6
1 X 500-g (18-oz) carton low-fat live natural yogurt (stirred yogurt combines better than set)
250 ml (8 fl oz) double cream
100 g (4 oz) caster sugar

Simply mix all the ingredients together and freeze in an ice-cream-making machine. Transfer to a suitable container and put in the freezer. If possible, remove from the freezer about 10 minutes before eating.

To make Summer Berry Frozen Yogurt, mix together 225 g (8 oz) fresh or frozen berries, eg: strawberries, raspberries, blueberries, blackberries. Gently simmer the fruit with a little sugar to taste, then liquidise in a blender and pass through a sieve. Mix the fruit purée with the yogurt mixture and freeze. Alternatively, purée and sieve 225 g (8 oz) fresh blueberries, raspberries or strawberries, beat in a little icing sugar and add to the yogurt mixture before freezing in an ice-cream-making machine.

Cookies and Cream Ice Cream

SERVES AS MANY AS YOU LIKE
vanilla ice cream

*Choose one of the following or try
making up your own flavour*
plain chocolate digestive biscuits
Oreo cookies
Maltesers
Dime chocolate bars
chopped dried fruit

It's easy to concoct your very own flavour of ice cream by mixing vanilla ice cream with your favourite biscuits or chocolate. My particular favourite is crushed oreo cookies (a very dark biscuit sandwiched together with vanilla cream) or vanilla ice cream and halva (which is a sweetmeat made with crushed sesame seeds)

Remove the ice cream from the fridge and allow to soften slightly. Place your chosen biscuits in a plastic bag and roughly crush with a rolling pin. Mash the crumbs into the ice cream and return to the freezer. Serve later in ice cream cones.

FRIDGE SKIPS

Fresh Fruit Cocktail Lollies

In summer my children love eating ice lollies made with fresh fruit. Naturally the success of your lollies will depend on the sweetness of the fruit you use. Try the combination below and then experiment making up your own flavours. Exotic fruits like passion fruit or mango are good ones to try.

Simply blend together all the fruits. Sieve the fruit purée and stir in the peach juice. Pour into ice lolly moulds and freeze.

VARIATION
The easiest way to make your own lollies is to pour fruit juice into lolly moulds. If you use contrasting coloured juices you can make two-tone ice lollies by freezing the first layer and pouring the second juice on top. Sometimes I add a little fresh fruit like a slice of strawberry or a raspberry.

MAKES 7 ICE LOLLIES
1 large orange, peeled and cut into
    segments with the pith removed
2 ripe peaches
2 slices of pineapple, cut into chunks
    and the hard core discarded
2 oranges
175 ml (6 fl oz) pure peach juice

Mini Milk Chocolate and Orange Lollies

MAKES 4 LOLLIES
50 g (2 oz) orange-flavoured milk
  chocolate
300 ml (½ pint) milk

Orange-flavoured milk chocolate, like the whole chocolate oranges that divide into segments which were one of my passions as a child, adds a delicious flavour to these milk-based ice lollies.

Simply add the chocolate broken into segments to the milk in a saucepan. Cook over a gentle heat, stirring until the chocolate has melted and flavoured the milk. Pour into ice-lolly moulds and freeze.

Peach Melba
Frozen Yogurt Lollies

So easy to make but children love them and they're much healthier than shop-bought ice lollies.

_____

Purée the raspberries and press through a sieve to get rid of the seeds. Blend together with the peach yogurt until smooth. Pour into lolly moulds and freeze.

MAKES 5 LOLLIES
100 g (4 oz) fresh raspberries
250 ml (8 fl oz) peach yogurt
(2 X 150 g/5 oz cartons)

Annabel's Apricot Cookies

Suitable for freezing
MAKES 26 COOKIES
100 g (4 oz) unsalted butter
100 g (4 oz) cream cheese
100 g (4 oz) caster sugar
75 g (3 oz) plain flour
50 g (2 oz) chopped dried apricots
65 g (2½ oz) white chocolate chips
   or chopped white chocolate

This fabulous and rather unusual combination of dried apricots and white chocolate makes irresistible cookies. Once you have sampled these you will probably want to double the quantities second time around.

In a large mixing bowl, cream together the butter and cream cheese. Add the sugar and beat until fluffy. Gradually add the flour, then fold in the apricots and chocolate. The dough will be quite soft – don't worry! Drop the mixture by heaped teaspoons on to baking sheets and bake in an oven preheated to 180°C/350°F/Gas 4 for 15 minutes or until lightly golden. Allow to cool and harden for a few minutes before removing them from the baking sheet.

Divinely Decadent Dark Chocolate and Apricot Bars

These no-bake chocolate fruit and nut bars are amazingly good and fun to make with your children but you will have to keep them hidden when Daddy comes home!

Break the chocolate into squares and put these in a dish together with the butter and microwave on Full power for 3 minutes, stirring halfway through, until melted. Alternatively, the chocolate can be melted in a bowl over a saucepan of simmering water. Stir the condensed milk into the chocolate mixture and mix in the broken biscuits, chopped apricots, raisins and chopped pecans. Line an 18 x 28-cm (7 x 11-inch) shallow cake tin with silver foil allowing the sides to overhang. Spoon the mixture into the tin, press down well and level out the surface. Set aside in the fridge to set. Once set, lift the cake out of the tin by the overhanging silver foil and cut into bars. Keep the bars chilled in the fridge.

Not suitable for freezing
MAKES 12 BARS
200 g (7 oz) good quality plain chocolate
75 g (3 oz) unsalted butter
1 x 397 g (14 oz) can condensed milk
225 g (8 oz) digestive biscuits, broken into pieces
100 g (4 oz) no-soak dried apricots, roughly chopped
50 g (2 oz) raisins
75 g (3 oz) pecans, roughly chopped

Glossy Dark and White Chocolate Brownies

Suitable for freezing
MAKES 16 SQUARES
150 g (5 oz) dark chocolate, chopped
75 g (3 oz) unsalted butter
5 ml (1 tsp) pure vanilla extract
100 g (4 oz) caster sugar
2 eggs
1 egg yolk
90 g (3½ oz) plain flour
1.25 ml (¼ tsp) salt
150 g (5 oz) white chocolate buttons or chopped white chocolate

CHOCOLATE SATIN GLAZE
75 g (3 oz) dark chocolate, chopped
15 g (½ oz) unsalted butter
50 g (2 oz) white chocolate buttons

Two different chocolates are combined together to make these irresistible little squares of rich, chewy brownies.

Melt the dark chocolate and butter in a microwave for 2 minutes on High (or in a saucepan over a gentle heat, stirring constantly). Stir in the vanilla and sugar, then add the eggs and yolk, one at a time, stirring after each addition. Sift together the flour and salt and mix this into the chocolate mixture with the chopped white chocolate. Pour the batter into a lined and greased 20-cm (8-inch) square baking pan and bake in an oven preheated to 180°C/350°F/Gas 4 for about 30 minutes.

TO PREPARE THE GLAZE, melt the dark chocolate and butter together and spread over the cake. Melt the white chocolate buttons and using a teaspoon trail 5 lines horizontally across the cake about 10cm (1 inch) apart. With a blunt knife draw vertical lines lightly through the chocolate topping to create a pattern.

Nicholas's After-School Biscuits

My son Nicholas, who is now eight years old, adores coming home and helping me out in the kitchen baking cakes or biscuits. Cooking is a great activity for children and I get him to measure out all the ingredients and then shape the mixture into little balls to be baked in the oven. The next morning he likes to take the biscuits to school to share with all his friends. These Anzac biscuits are traditional Australian biscuits and are very simple and quick to make.

Not suitable for freezing
MAKES 30 BISCUITS
100 g (4 oz) butter
30 ml (2 tbsp) golden syrup
100 g (4 oz) caster sugar
75 g (3 oz) desiccated coconut
75 g (3 oz) rolled oats
100 g (4 oz) plain flour
5 ml (1 tsp) baking soda
30 ml (2 tbsp) boiling water

Melt the butter and golden syrup together in a large saucepan. Mix together the sugar, coconut, rolled oats and flour. Dissolve the baking soda in the boiling water and stir into the melted butter mixture. Stir in the dry ingredients and form into about 3.5 cm (1½ inch) small balls. Arrange on a greased baking tray, pressing down gently to flatten and bake in an oven preheated to 180°C/350°F/Gas 4 for 15 to 20 minutes or until golden. Allow to cool and harden on a rack before eating.

Muffin If Not Delicious

Suitable for freezing
MAKES 12 MUFFINS
75 g (3 oz) butter
280 g (10 oz) plain flour
10 ml (2 tsp) baking powder
2.5 ml (½ tsp) baking soda
2.5 ml (½ tsp) salt
2.5 ml (½ tsp) ground cinnamon
1.25 ml (¼ tsp) ground ginger
1 egg
125 g (4½ oz) soft brown sugar
350 ml (12 fl oz) milk
350 g (12 fl oz) canned pumpkin
75 g (3 oz) raisins

My special ingredient for these delicious muffins is canned pumpkin which keeps them very moist and gives a lovely flavour. I don't think many people would be able to guess they contain pumpkin and it's quite fun asking people to eat one and see if they can tell you what they are made from.

Melt the butter and set aside to cool. Meanwhile, sift together all the dry ingredients. Mix together the melted butter, lightly beaten egg, sugar and milk until combined and stir in the pumpkin and raisins. Fold in the dry ingredients until just mixed. Put 12 paper cases for muffins in a muffin tray and spoon in the mixture. Bake at 200°C/400°F/Gas 6 for 20 to 25 minutes.

Apple and Cinnamon Muffins with a Crunchy Topping

The crunchy cinnamon topping sets off these lovely moist apple muffins.

Sift together the flour, baking soda, cinnamon and salt. Beat the sugar and oil with an electric mixer and gradually beat in the egg and vanilla. Fold in the sifted dry ingredients and then mix in the chopped apple and raisins. Spoon the batter into a muffin tray lined with paper cases.

TO MAKE THE CRUNCHY TOPPING, rub together all the ingredients with your fingertips until the mixture resembles large crumbs and gently press these on top of the batter. Bake in an oven preheated to 180°C/350°F/Gas 4 for about 30 minutes. The crumbs should be crunchy and the muffins lightly golden.

Not suitable for freezing
MAKES 12 MUFFINS
100 g (4 oz) plain flour
2.5 ml (½ tsp) baking soda
2.5 ml (½ tsp) ground cinnamon
1.25 ml (¼ tsp) salt
150 g (5 oz) caster sugar
120 ml (4 fl oz) vegetable oil
1 egg
5 ml (1 tsp) pure vanilla extract
1 large Granny Smith apple, peeled
   and chopped
30 ml (2 tbsp) raisins

CRUNCHY TOPPING
50 g (2 oz) plain flour
25 g (1 oz) brown sugar
25 g (1 oz) unsalted butter
1.25 ml (¼ tsp) ground cinnamon

Funny Face Fairy Cakes

Suitable for freezing
MAKES 10 CUPCAKES
100 g (4 oz) soft unsalted
   butter
90 g (3½ oz) caster sugar
2 eggs
2.5 ml (½ tsp) vanilla essence
100 g (4 oz) self-raising flour

ICING
175 g (6 oz) icing sugar
water
a few drops of food colouring
   (optional)
small tubes of coloured Writing Icing
Mini Liquorice Allsorts and assorted
   sweets

OPTIONAL EXTRAS
To make Plump Raisin Cupcakes add
   75 g (3 oz) raisins or sultanas
To make Cherry Cupcakes add 50 g
   (2 oz) desiccated coconut and 75 g
   (3 oz) chopped glacé cherries
   (rinse cherries first and dust with a
   little flour)
To make Chocolate Cupcakes add
   25 g (1 oz) sifted cocoa
   powder

These are always very popular at children's birthday parties, decorated with faces made from miniature Liquorice Allsorts and various other sweets. My children adore making these with me in the kitchen and designing their own funny faces. You can also make miniature fairy cakes for young children using paper cases for confectionery and baking the cakes in a mini-muffin tin.

Beat the butter and sugar together until light and creamy. Lightly beat the eggs with the vanilla and add them to the butter mixture a little at a time. Gradually fold in the flour and any optional extras. Line two bun tins with paper cases and spoon the batter into the cases until about two-thirds full. Bake in an oven preheated to 180°C/350°F/Gas 4 for about 15 minutes or until a cocktail stick inserted into the centre comes out clean.

TO MAKE THE ICING, sift the icing sugar into a bowl and stir in a little water (or lemon juice) gradually to make a thick smooth paste. If you wish, colour the icing with a few drops of edible food colouring. Once the cakes are cool, ice and decorate them.

Lara's Cooking-Party Birthday

For Lara's seventh birthday I wanted to do something rather unusual and came up with the idea of having a 'Cooking Party' since all my children love helping me cook in the kitchen. With the help of two young girls, Venetia and Jane, who organise birthday cooking parties called Cookie Crumble Parties, Lara invited 20 of her friends and chose five fun recipes to make for tea. All the children were given chef's hats with their names printed on them, aprons and wooden spoons and where appropriate all the ingredients were weighed out in the morning to save time. We explained to the children, one stage at a time, what they should do and they set about making the recipes in pairs, with the adults supervising and baking the finished creations in the oven. Everyone had a great time and everybody, especially Mummy, got quite messy. It was certainly a novelty for the children to sit down to a tea that they had cooked themselves and they all tucked in with gusto!!

Since the party was such a great success, I thought I would share with you three of the recipes the children made so that you could have your own cooking party one day. You could make it a holiday treat to invite a group of your children's friends over and have a cooking afternoon where the children prepare their own tea or even supper. The five recipes that Lara chose for her party were Pizza Faces, Cheesy Feet, Animal Biscuits, Chocolate Hedgehogs and Chocolate Milkshake with ice cream. We also managed two games of pass the parcel which kept the children occupied while we cleared the tables halfway through.

Pizza Faces

Suitable for freezing
MAKES 2 PIZZA FACES
100 g (4 oz) self-raising flour
generous pinch of salt
25 g (1 oz) butter, cut into small pieces
40 g (1½ oz) grated Cheddar cheese
30–45 ml (2–3 tbsp) milk, to bind
30 ml (2 tbsp) tomato pizza sauce
30–45 ml (2–3 tbsp) grated
    mozzarella cheese or 2 cheese
    slices
toppings, eg: canned sweetcorn,
    sliced button mushrooms, stoned
    black olives, peperoni etc.

Set the oven to 220°C/425°F/Gas 7. Place the flour, salt and butter into a bowl and rub with your fingertips until it looks like breadcrumbs. Add the grated cheese and milk and mix until the mixture becomes a smooth ball of dough. Divide the dough in half, sprinkle some flour on the table and roll out the dough to the size of a saucer. Spread the pizza sauce on top of the dough and sprinkle the cheese on top. Decorate the pizzas and lay them on a greased baking tray. Bake for 15 to 20 minutes or until the edges are golden brown.

Cheesy Feet

Y ou will need to make templates of feet using a sheet of plastic or card for the children to cut around. Alternatively, you could use biscuit cutters (like animal shapes) to cut out different cheese pastry shapes.

_____

Grease a large baking tray with the butter and set the oven to 200°C/400°F/Gas 6. Sprinkle the table with a little flour and roll out the pastry with a rolling pin. Prick it with a fork to stop it rising during the cooking. Place the foot template on the pastry and cut around it. Beat the egg with a fork and brush over the pastry. Sprinkle with the cheese. Lift the feet very carefully on to a greased baking tray and cut out little pieces of tomato and decorate the toes with red toenails. Bake for 10 to 15 minutes then cool on a wire rack.

Suitable for freezing
MAKES 4
25 g (1 oz) butter
100 g (4 oz) JusRoll puff pastry sheets
   (frozen uncooked pastry sheets,
   defrosted)
1 egg
100 g (4 oz) grated cheese
1 tomato or 5 ml (1 tsp) tomato
   purée

Chocolate Hedgehogs

Suitable for freezing
MAKES 10 CHOCOLATE
HEDGEHOGS
100 g (4 oz) caster sugar
100 g (4 oz) soft butter
2 eggs
100 g (4 oz) self-raising flour
25 g (1 oz) raisins (optional)
chocolate buttons and dolly mixture
    for decoration

CHOCOLATE FROSTING
100 g (4 oz) butter
200 g (7 oz) icing sugar
30 ml (2 tbsp) cocoa powder
30 ml (2 tbsp) milk

This is the first recipe the children should prepare, since the cakes will need time to cool down before they are iced. It works best to divide the ingredients for baking and icing the fairy cakes in half, ie: 1 egg, 50 g sugar etc., so that each pair will make 5 little cakes which they can then decorate.

Beat the sugar and butter together until light and fluffy. Beat the eggs into the mixture one at a time, then add the flour and stir until well blended. If you are adding raisins, fold them in now. Line a bun tray with paper cases and spoon some of the mixture into each paper case. Preheat the oven to 180°C/350°F/Gas 4 and bake the cakes for about 20 minutes. Put on a wire rack to cool. While the cakes are in the oven prepare the chocolate frosting. Beat the butter until soft, sieve together the icing sugar and cocoa and beat into the butter together with the milk. When the cakes have cooled, spread a thick layer of chocolate frosting on to each cake and decorate with halved chocolate buttons for spikes and dolly mixture for the eyes and nose.

There are a number of other recipes in this book which would also be suitable to include in a cooking party, for example: 10-Minute French Bread Pizza (p.151), Noughts and Crosses (p.150), Funny Face Fairy Cakes (p.184), Apple Smiles (p.153).

Index

Acknowledgements

I am indebted to the following people for their help and advice during the writing of this book.

Evelyn Etkind, my greatest supporter, for sharing my triumphs and disasters in the kitchen and joining me in eating all manner of strange concoctions at all hours of the day and night, sequestering the best of these for her own private dinner parties.

Simon, my husband, the source of my greatest inspiration who was there at the beginning and who has uncomplainingly been the final recipient of nearly all the recipes in this book. A stern critic whose changing physique amply testifies to his liking of my recipes for children's food. Be grateful, my darling, that this is not a book of baby purees!

David Karmel whose computer mouse has been invaluable and has prevented me from getting cheesed off.

Jane Hamilton, my nanny, who made it possible for me to write this book and whose sweet tooth has been amply rewarded for duty of care.

Beryl Lewsey, a great 'exhibitionist', organiser and sounding board.

Marian A. Magpoc, for her invaluable help and for the oriental spice she has added to this book.

Letty A. Catada, for her smiling face and the other pair of hands in my kitchen.

Jacqui Morley, for her support whilst writing this book.

Susan Hellard, for bringing my recipes to life with such humour.

Luci Daniels BSc Hon, State Registered Dietician, for checking through my manuscript with a fine toothcomb.

Cosmo Place Studios for the loan of the china in the photographs.

Joanna Sheehan, Martin Lovelock and Fiona Eves for helping to transform my recipes and ideas into this beautiful book.

Also by Annabel Karmel

ISBN: 0 09 175104 7 £10.99

ISBN: 0 09 178354 2 £10.99

ISBN: 0 09 186373 2 £10.99

ISBN: 0 09 186084 9 £10.99

All are published by Ebury Press and available from all good bookshops.
Alternatively, call our credit card hotline on 01206 255 800
(postage and packaging are free)